JOSEPH CONRAD

THE GREENHAVEN PRESS

Literary Companion

TO BRITISH AUTHORS

JOSEPH CONRAD

David Bender, *Publisher*

Bruno Leone, *Executive Editor*

Brenda Stalcup, *Managing Editor*

Bonnie Szumski, *Series Editor*

Clarice Swisher, *Book Editor*

Every effort has been made to trace the owners of copyrighted material. The articles in this volume may have been edited for content, length, and/or reading level. The titles have been changed to enhance the editorial purpose of the Opposing Viewpoints® concept. Those interested in locating the original source will find the complete citation on the first page of each article.

Library of Congress Cataloging-in-Publication Data

Readings on Joseph Conrad / Clarice Swisher, book editor.
     p.   cm. — (The Greenhaven Press literary companion to British authors)
   Includes bibliographical references and index.
   ISBN 1-56510-637-7 (lib. bdg. : alk. paper). —
ISBN 1-56510-636-9 (pbk. : alk. paper)
   1. Conrad, Joseph, 1857–1924—Criticism and interpretation. I. Swisher, Clarice, 1933–   . II. Series.
PR6005.04Z78656   1998
823'.912—dc21   97-4350
                                                                              CIP

Cover photo: UPI/Bettmann

Copyright ©1998 by Greenhaven Press, Inc.
PO Box 289009
San Diego, CA 92198-9009
Printed in the U.S.A.

"Give me the right word and the right accent and I will move the world."

—*Joseph Conrad,* A Personal Record

CONTENTS

Chapter 1: Conrad's Themes and Methods

1. The Prose Writer's Goals and Methods
by Joseph Conrad
A prose writer captures a moment in the work and actions
of individual characters. If the writer is successful, the art
stirs the emotions and offers a glimpse into the truth of life.

2. Conrad Learns His Craft *by Walter F. Wright*
Conrad vigorously pursued the art of writing stories and
novels by studying other writers' views and techniques.
With discipline and imagination, he learned to create a
new reality out of his personal experiences and to use
symbols and metaphors to express universal ideas.

3. Major Elements in Conrad's Stories
by Jerry Allen
Works throughout Conrad's career exhibit common elements. For most of his stories, Conrad draws on his sea experiences for similar plots, characters, and themes; his approach to the subject is what changed as he matured.

4. Conrad as Painter *by Adam Gillon*
Because Conrad creates a profusion of concrete images,
his prose can be likened to paintings. In *Lord Jim*, Conrad
paints a portrait of Jim, starting with a broad outline,
adding details of his appearance, and filling in with images that indicate the inner man.

5. Gender Roles in Conrad's Novels *by Cedric Watts*
On the literal level, Conrad portrays men and women in
the traditional roles of a patriarchal society, but he was
ahead of his time in that his underlying psychological interpretations often depict injustices in that system.

Chapter 2: Conrad's Short Works

1. Imagination and Character in *Typhoon*
by Jeremy Hawthorn
In *Typhoon,* Conrad explores the theme of imagination

through the character of Captain MacWhirr, a literal-minded man interested only in facts. When the captain's ship is threatened by a typhoon, he gains sympathy and the understanding of what is *possible*, not merely of what *is*.

Chapter 3: Conrad's Early Novels, 1897–1900

FOREWORD

*"'Tis the good reader that
makes the good book."*

Ralph Waldo Emerson

The story's bare facts are simple: The captain, an old and scarred seafarer, walks with a peg leg made of whale ivory. He relentlessly drives his crew to hunt the world's oceans for the great white whale that crippled him. After a long search, the ship encounters the whale and a fierce battle ensues. Finally the captain drives his harpoon into the whale, but the harpoon line catches the captain about the neck and drags him to his death.

A simple story, a straightforward plot—yet, since the 1851 publication of Herman Melville's *Moby-Dick*, readers and critics have found many meanings in the struggle between Captain Ahab and the whale. To some, the novel is a cautionary tale that depicts how Ahab's obsession with revenge leads to his insanity and death. Others believe that the whale represents the unknowable secrets of the universe and that Ahab is a tragic hero who dares to challenge fate by attempting to discover this knowledge. Perhaps Melville intended Ahab as a criticism of Americans' tendency to become involved in well-intentioned but irrational causes. Or did Melville model Ahab after himself, letting his fictional character express his anger at what he perceived as a cruel and distant god?

Although literary critics disagree over the meaning of *Moby-Dick*, readers do not need to choose one particular interpretation in order to gain an understanding of Melville's novel. Instead, by examining various analyses, they can gain numerous insights into the issues that lie under the surface of the basic plot. Studying the writings of literary critics can also aid readers in making their own assessments of *Moby-Dick* and other literary works and in developing analytical thinking skills.

The Greenhaven Literary Companion Series was created with these goals in mind. Designed for young adults, this unique anthology series provides an engaging and comprehensive introduction to literary analysis and criticism. The essays included in the Literary Companion Series are chosen for their accessibility to a young adult audience and are expertly edited in consideration of both the reading and comprehension levels of this audience. In addition, each essay is introduced by a concise summation that presents the contributing writer's main themes and insights. Every anthology in the Literary Companion Series contains a varied selection of critical essays that cover a wide time span and express diverse views. Wherever possible, primary sources are represented through excerpts from authors' notebooks, letters, and journals and through contemporary criticism.

Each title in the Literary Companion Series pays careful consideration to the historical context of the particular author or literary work. In-depth biographies and detailed chronologies reveal important aspects of authors' lives and emphasize the historical events and social milieu that influenced their writings. To facilitate further research, every anthology includes primary and secondary source bibliographies of articles and/or books selected for their suitability for young adults. These engaging features make the Greenhaven Literary Companion series ideal for introducing students to literary analysis in the classroom or as a library resource for young adults researching the world's great authors and literature.

Exceptional in its focus on young adults, the Greenhaven Literary Companion Series strives to present literary criticism in a compelling and accessible format. Every title in the series is intended to spark readers' interest in leading American and world authors, to help them broaden their understanding of literature, and to encourage them to formulate their own analyses of the literary works that they read. It is the editors' hope that young adult readers will find these anthologies to be true companions in their study of literature.

INTRODUCTION

James E. Miller Jr., a Conrad critic, has said that students who have a passion for reading naturally learn "most of the elements fundamental to growth in language and composition." But through literature they learn "about life, reality, experience, themselves, and their society. . . . And what they know they will know in ways possible by no other means." Joseph Conrad wrote novels and stories about "life, reality, experience" at its deepest levels. In a letter to the *New York Times,* Conrad wrote: "The only legitimate basis of creative work lies in the courageous recognition of all the irreconcilable antagonisms that make our life so enigmatic, so burdensome, so fascinating, so dangerous, so full of hope. They exist! And this is the only fundamental truth of fiction." He expressed himself not in a straightforward record of action and dialogue but in an imaginative unfolding of impressions, in a dreamlike pattern. For the student and ordinary reader, grasping Conrad's themes and understanding his method of expression are difficult; critical analysis and opinion can be a particularly helpful tool.

This volume comprises a variety of criticism. Some contributors are respected scholars who have studied Conrad's works for many years. Others are recent critics writing with a new perspective. Conrad himself explains his intent as a writer in one essay, and another is written by a novelist and dramatist.

Readings on Joseph Conrad includes many special features that make research and literary criticism accessible and understandable. An annotated table of contents lets readers quickly preview the contents of individual essays. A chronology features a list of significant events in Conrad's life placed in a broader historical context. The bibliography includes books on Conrad's time and additional critical sources suitable for further research.

Each essay has aids for clear understanding. Individual

introductions serve to explain the main points, which are then identified by subheads within the essays. Footnotes explain uncommon references and define unfamiliar words. Taken together, these aids make the Greenhaven Press *Literary Companion Series* an indispensable research tool.

Joseph Conrad: A Biography

"I am another kind of person," Joseph Conrad wrote to his agent. Though Conrad was responding to a particular misunderstanding, the line characterizes Conrad professionally and personally. Conrad, an orphan by age eleven, grew up in Poland speaking Polish, yet became a major British novelist and short story writer who wrote all his works in English. For fifteen years, he worked on British merchant ships before becoming a writer. He wrote romantic stories of energy and adventure. "I am modern," he repeated to those who misjudged his work.

Jozef Teodor Konrad Nalecz Korzeniowski was born on December 3, 1857, in Berdichev in the Polish Ukraine, a hundred miles southwest of Kiev. His father, Apollo Korzeniowski, educated in Oriental languages, law, and literature at St. Petersburg University, was a writer and translator. As a Polish patriot, Apollo believed in sacrifice for one's country and led others in political causes. Conrad's mother, Ewelina Bobrowska, called Eva, thirteen years younger than Apollo, was a warm, imaginative woman who loved Apollo and chose him in spite of her parents' disapproval. Both Eva and Apollo were members of the *szlachta*, the ruling class. While Eva's father ignored politics and focused his attention on increasing his wealth, the Korzeniowskis devoted time, energy, and money to the revolutionary cause.

Conrad's Disrupted Childhood

Apollo's political activities profoundly affected Conrad's childhood. In 1795 Poland's neighbors, threatened by Poland's liberal constitution, partitioned the country. Russia annexed the central and eastern territory; Poland retained the western part until 1830, when Prussia acquired it; and the southern part was incorporated into the Austrian Empire. When Napoleon invaded Russia in the early 1800s, Poles expected reunification, but the division remained. After two failed revolutions in 1830 and 1846, another uprising was brewing in the early 1860s. Apollo, who resisted oppressive Russian rule and provoked authorities by his dress and his radical agitation for resistance, was arrested and imprisoned for seven months. While he awaited trial, Eva took Conrad, age three, to see his father through the prison window. Apollo was found guilty and exiled; Eva and Conrad traveled with him to Vologda, 250 miles north of Moscow, where they survived the cold winter on meager rations. From this experience, all three of them became sick; Eva developed tuberculosis and died on April 18, 1865, when Conrad was seven. He was devastated by his mother's death, and Apollo assumed guilt for his arrest, their exile, and the death of his wife. Conrad, a frail child, became nervous and unstable and often ill; his unhealthy state continued into adult life.

After Eva's death, Conrad lived in lonely, sad isolation with Apollo, who had also contracted tuberculosis. Aside from a brief stay with his grandmother in Kiev to recuperate from illness, Conrad took care of his sick father. Because Apollo wanted nothing of the hated Russians and their culture to influence his son, he kept him out of school and away from other children and taught Conrad himself. To escape loneliness and the stress of his demanding father's instruction, Conrad immersed himself in reading. Apollo wrote of his son:

> Poor child: he does not know what a contemporary playmate is; he looks at the decrepitude of my sadness and who knows if that sight does not make his young heart wrinkled or his awakening soul grizzled. These are important reasons for forcing me to tear the poor child away from my dejected heart. . . .

> Since last autumn my health has been declining badly and my dear little mite takes care of me. . . .

> My life is, at present, confined solely to Konradek. I teach him all I know myself—alas, it is not much; I guard him against the influence of the local atmosphere and the little mite is growing up as though in a cloister.

Prince Galitzen, the governor of Chernikhov, saw that Apollo was dying after five and a half years in Russia, and no longer a threat to the government. Released, father and son moved to Lvov and then to Kraków in southern Poland. By this time, Apollo's health had worsened; he said to a friend, "I am broken, fit for nothing, too tired even to spit upon things." Conrad watched his father's slow decline from tuberculosis until May 13, 1869, when Apollo died. His funeral brought out several thousand patriotic Poles whom eleven-year-old Conrad led in a procession through the streets to the burial site. In *Joseph Conrad: A Biography*, Jeffrey Meyers describes the role model Apollo had provided for his son as "a volatile temperament, an anguished patriotism, the bitterness of shattered hopes, the trauma of defeat and a deep-rooted pessimism." Thirty years later, however, Conrad remembered his father more generously:

> A man of great sensibilities; of exalted and dreamy temperament; with a terrible gift of irony and of gloomy disposition; withal of strong religious feelings degenerating after the loss of his wife into mysticism touched with despair. His aspect was distinguished; his conversation very fascinating; his face in repose somber, lighted all over when he [rarely] smiled. I remember him well. For the last two years of his life I lived alone with him.

CONRAD THE ORPHAN

Conrad the orphan was placed under the guardianship of his doting grandmother Theophila Bobrowska and his uncle Count Ladislaw Mniszek, but it was Conrad's uncle Thaddeus, Eva's widowed brother, who took over full responsibility for his nephew. He sent Conrad to a small school run by Mr. Louis Georgeon in Kraków. During the summer of 1870, Thaddeus hired Adam Pulman to tutor Conrad in Latin and German so that he could enter St. Jacek's gymnasium, but Conrad lacked the discipline to meet the rigorous curriculum. In *Joseph Conrad: A Critical Biography*, Jocelyn Baines explains Conrad's poor school performance:

> Conrad seems to have disliked school-life, and it is not surprising, in view of his unorthodox upbringing, that he should have found the unaccustomed discipline of regular work irksome. It is probable, too, that academically he was by temperament lazy. . . . Apollo had earlier found that he "showed no love of study." Apparently he liked always to be untrammelled, and at school or at home preferred to lounge rather than sit.

Thaddeus then sent the fifteen-year-old Conrad to a boardinghouse for orphans of the 1863 insurrection, a place run by a distant cousin, Antony Syroczynski. Conrad, who had spent his childhood with adults, made friends with three boys in nearby apartments and found girls and love. He met Janina Taube, whose rejection wounded Conrad's ego, and fell in love with Tekla Syroczynski. Conrad later wrote about his first loves in *The Arrow of Gold.*

During this period Conrad determined to go to sea. His romantic longing for the sea grew out of his boyhood reading of sea adventures, including those by Victor Hugo, James Fenimore Cooper, and Frederick Marryat. Conrad loved and studied geography at the expense of his other school subjects, once pointing at the Congo saying he wanted to go there. Moreover, he wanted to leave Poland. The relatives finally consented to allow him to join the French merchant navy, and Conrad at seventeen years old left on a train for the Mediterranean French seaport of Marseilles in October 1874.

CONRAD'S FRENCH EXPERIENCES

Conrad's uncle Thaddeus gave him an allowance and arranged contacts in Marseilles. Conrad was fortunate to meet people who offered him a social life as well as a job. He met the ship-owning family the Delestangs; they included Conrad in their cultural events and introduced him to artists and intellectuals who became his friends.

Conrad also met Baptistin, a cousin of the Delestangs. As friends the two young men explored the night life of the city. Baptistin brought Conrad to the harbor where he developed friendships with the seamen who worked on pilot boats used to guide ships into harbor. Accepted by the sailors, Conrad was invited to join them; he wrote in his memoirs:

> The very first whole day I ever spent on salt water was by invitation, in a big half-decked pilot-boat, cruising under close reefs on the lookout, in misty, blowing weather, for the sails of ships and the smoke of steamers rising out there, beyond the slim and tall Planier lighthouse cutting the line of the wind-swept horizon with a white perpendicular stroke. They were hospitable souls, these sturdy Provencal seamen. Under the general designation of *le petit ami de Baptistin* I was made the guest of the Corporation of Pilots, and had the freedom of their boats night and day.

Two months after arriving in Marseilles, Conrad made the first of three voyages on ships owned by the Delestangs. He traveled first as a passenger on the *Mont Blanc* to Martinique in the Caribbean, leaving Marseilles on December 11, 1874, and returning on May 12, 1875. In *The Mirror of the Sea*, Conrad describes a storm near the Straits of Gibraltar: "The very first Christmas night I ever spent away from land was employed in running before a Gulf of Lyons gale, which made the old ship groan in every timber. . . . I listened for the first time with the curiosity of my tender years to the song of the wind in the ship's rigging." On a second voyage in June 1875, Conrad traveled again on the *Mont Blanc* to Martinique, but this time he served as an apprentice seaman. The return winter voyage was stormy, and the ship needed repair when it reached Le Havre, France, on December 23, 1875. Conrad left the ship and took the train to Marseilles, stopping in Paris for a few days on the way. On his third voyage, Conrad served as a steward, earning thirty-five francs a month, on a bigger, newer ship, *Saint Antoine*, which left Marseilles on July 8, 1876. Besides Martinique, the *Saint Antoine* docked in Colombia, Venezuela, St. Thomas, and Haiti before its return on February 15, 1877. This voyage provided Conrad with glimpses of South America that he would use as the setting for *Nostromo*. He also met first mate Dominic Cervone, who became the model for major characters in three novels.

Conrad, now nineteen, spent the year from February 1877 to the following February living extravagantly and recklessly in Marseilles. He attended operas and enjoyed the company of his bohemian friends in the cafés. He joined the Carlists, a political faction involved in civil war in Spain, to which he and a few partners smuggled guns from the coves near Marseilles to the northeast corner of Spain. What was an adventure to Conrad ended when a Spanish patrol boat gave chase and the captain of the smuggling crew ran their boat aground near shore to let the crew escape. During the year, Conrad had made plans for another voyage on the *Saint Antoine:* Too sick to leave on the departure date, he waited for the fall voyage, but when the time came, the French military forbade him to go because Conrad had failed to obtain a permit from the Russian consul releasing him from military duty. With the three thousand francs Thaddeus had given him for the voyage, Conrad linked up with the captain of the *Mont Blanc,* who persuaded Conrad to invest in a scheme involving contraband. Conrad lost the entire three thousand francs, borrowed eight hundred francs from a friend to try to make up for the loss in the Monte Carlo casino, and lost there, too. He had no money and could never again sail on a French ship. In his depression and desperation, he attempted suicide by shooting himself in the chest, but the bullet missed all important organs, and Conrad recovered in a few days. A circulated story claimed that Conrad had been shot in a duel, but Conrad supposedly told his uncle that he had pulled the trigger.

During Conrad's years in Marseilles, his uncle Thaddeus provided him with money, advice, and emotional support. Though Thaddeus sent money when Conrad lost it, over-spent, or gambled it away, it came with scoldings and advice in long letters spelling out proper attitudes and behavior. Typical in tone is one letter Conrad received after losing his trunk and family photographs:

> You have always, my dear fellow, annoyed me with your lack of order and your carefree treatment of things—in which you remind me of the Korzeniowski family—always wasting everything—and not of my dear sister, your mother, so painstaking in everything. Last year, you lost your trunk with your things: what else was there to have in mind during a journey except yourself and your things? Now, again you have lost your family photographs and Polish books, and you want me to make up a set of one and the other! What for: So that you may again lose them at the first opportunity!! . . . So, if you don't care for cherished souvenirs (for there's no ac-counting for tastes, and such do exist), why clamour for them and cause others trouble? . . .

> Well, there's your scolding for your lack of order in preserving your property. You really deserve a second one; for your untidy way of writing letters—I've written about this several times. Is it impossible to have a supply of paper with you and to write decently? I sincerely wish my nephew to be a decent man and that's why I scold him—though this doesn't prevent me from loving you and blessing you, my dear boy—and this I do.

> Embracing you heartily, your uncle
> T. Bobrowski

As one can tell from the tone of this letter, strictness did not come easily to Thaddeus. No matter how his nephew be-haved, Thaddeus remained a loving and devoted uncle. In March 1878 Thaddeus received a telegram saying *"Conrad blesse, envoyez argent—arrivez"* ["Conrad wounded, send money—come"]. Thaddeus arrived in Marseilles on March 11, stayed two weeks, and paid Conrad's debts, doctor bills, and rent. But his love and generosity were not without this scolding: "You were idling for nearly a whole year—you fell into debt, you deliberately shot yourself. . . . Really, you have exceeded the limits of stupidity permitted to your age!"

The end of Conrad's stay in France marked a turning point in his life. He had learned French, his second lan-guage, and was about to leave his irresponsible, inconsider-ate, passionate, depression-prone youth behind. His friend Richard Fecht helped him join a British merchant ship, and

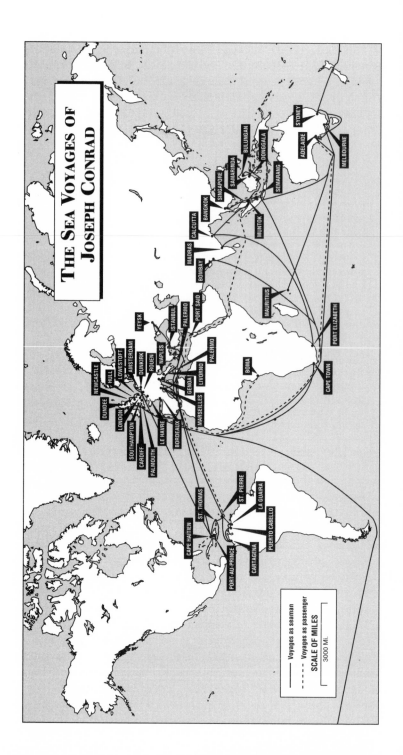

THE SEA VOYAGES OF
JOSEPH CONRAD

Voyages as seaman
Voyages as passenger
SCALE OF MILES
3000 Mi.

on April 24, 1878, Conrad embarked on the *Mavis,* a British freighter hauling coal to Constantinople. As a child in Poland, Conrad had vowed, "if a seaman, then an English seaman"; he had his first chance on the *Mavis.*

CONRAD BECOMES AN ENGLISH SEAMAN

Conrad reached England for the first time on June 18, 1878, when the *Mavis* docked at Lowestoft. He was twenty, alone and a stranger, and he spoke only a few words of English. During the next fifteen years, he would sail on seventeen ships to ports across Europe, Asia, Africa, and Australia.

Conrad worked his way from ordinary seaman to master seaman and became a naturalized British citizen during his navy career. He took and passed the exam to become second mate in June 1880. During the winter of 1884, Conrad passed the first-mate exam. Conrad became a British subject on August 19, 1886, and a month later his uncle wrote, "I am extremely glad that you have completed your naturalization, and clasp my Englishman to my breast as well as my nephew." Three months later, on November 10, Conrad passed the examination for a master's certificate, which allowed him to be the captain of a ship. This exam required knowledge of winds, currents, navigation, nautical astronomy, instruments, and measurements, much of which required mathematical calculations. His uncle wrote an ecstatic reply to his nephew's achievement: "Long live the *'Ordin: Master British Merchant Service'!* May he live as long as possible! May he be healthy and may every success meet him in every enterprise on sea and on land!" Conrad's reaction, however, was more subdued. He recalls in *A Personal Record:*

> It was a fact, I said to myself, that I was now a British master mariner beyond a doubt. It was not that I had an exaggerated sense of that very modest achievement, with which, however, luck, opportunity, or any extraneous influence could have had nothing to do. That fact, satisfactory and obscure in itself, had for me a certain ideal significance.

He felt he had now proved he could amount to something.

Though Conrad took no notes, captains and fellow seamen, events onboard ships, and impressions of places implanted themselves in his mind, later to become part of his novels. In *Joseph Conrad: The Three Lives: A Biography,* Frederick R. Karl notes the nature of a seaman's career—hard work, poor food, inconvenience, and unsanitary conditions:

Perhaps we fail to recognize how sheerly dangerous sailoring was, how close to drowning Conrad was, and how the "romance of the sea" was intermixed with the claims of the sea, those ships and crews who went down, marginal to the last.

THE CONGO EXPERIENCE

Unable to find a job on an English ship in 1889, Conrad took a job in the Congo with a Belgian company, fulfilling his childhood vow, "When I grow up, I shall go there." Conrad was to take a boat forty miles up the Congo River to an outpost of the ivory trade. Once there, he was assigned to the *Roi des Belges* to learn the river and to assist the captain in rescuing a seriously ill company agent. On the way, the captain fell ill and Conrad had to take over. They rescued the agent, who died on the way downriver, the captain survived, and Conrad got so sick that the illness undermined his health permanently, making him susceptible to fevers and pain in the joints for the rest of his life. What Conrad saw of colonialism and the ivory trade on that trip upriver appalled him. He wrote in his diary:

> They were no colonists; their administration was merely a squeeze and nothing more, I suspect. They were conquerors, and for that you want only brute force—nothing to boast of, when you have it, since your strength is just an accident arising from the weakness of others. They grabbed what they could get for the sake of what was to be got. It was just robbery with violence, aggravated murder on a great scale, and men going at it blind—as is very proper for those who tackle a darkness. The conquest of the earth, which mostly means the taking it away from those who have a different complexion or slightly flatter noses than ourselves, is not a pretty thing when you look into it too much.

This trip formed the basis for "Heart of Darkness" which, Conrad said, "pushed a little (only a little) beyond the actual facts of the case." Conrad returned to England in January 1891 and entered a London hospital to recover. He was sick, out of work, and depressed.

CONRAD BEGINS TO WRITE

For a short time Conrad's sea career, which was losing its appeal, overlapped his writing, which increasingly interested him. He had written his first story, "The Black Mate," in 1886 for a competition sponsored by a magazine. He wrote nothing more until 1889 when he started *Almayer's Folly,* which, he claims in *A Personal Record*, began without intention:

> I never made a note of a fact, of an impression or of an anec-
> dote in my life. The conception of a planned book was entirely
> outside my mental range when I sat down to write; the ambi-
> tion of being an author had never turned up amongst these
> gracious imaginary existences one creates fondly for oneself at
> times in the stillness and immobility of a day-dream.

Conrad worked on *Almayer's Folly* for three years. In July
1894 he sent the completed manuscript under the pseudo-
nym Kamudi to the publisher Fisher Unwin, who bought it
for £20 and published it. All reviews were encouraging, especially noting Conrad's adventurous use of language; H.G.
Wells wrote in the *Saturday Review* that it was "exceedingly
well imagined and well written, and it will certainly secure
Mr. Conrad a high place among contemporary story tellers."

In October that year Conrad met Edward Garnett, a
reader for Unwin, who encouraged Conrad to write another
novel. Conrad, who began *An Outcast of the Islands* the
evening after his conversation with Garnett, set it in the
same area of the Pacific Islands as *Almayer's Folly*, used
many of the same characters, and addressed themes of betrayal and retribution. Published in 1896, *An Outcast* got
many good reviews; H.G. Wells, writing in the *Saturday Review*, criticized Conrad's wordiness but thought it the best
book published in that year. Of Conrad he said, "He writes so
as to mask and dishonor the greatness in him. Greatness is
deliberately written. . . . Only greatness could make books of
which the detailed workmanship was so copiously bad, so
well worth reading, so convincing, and so stimulating."

Conrad was often asked why he wrote in English rather
than in his native Polish or in French. Jokingly he explained
that "I value our beautiful [Polish] literature too highly to introduce into it my inept fumbling." By the time Conrad wrote his
first novel, he had been speaking English for eleven years. Conrad had learned conversational English from the fishermen
and sailors in a little inn in Lowestoft where he stayed between
voyages. Analyses of the sentences in the newspaper *Standard*,
the only literature in the seaport town, were his first lessons in
English. Conrad learned literary English by studying Shakespeare's plays and Lord Byron's poems aboard ship. He explained to his friend Hugh Walpole in 1918:

> When I wrote the first words of *Almayer's Folly*, I had been al-
> ready for years and years *thinking* in English. I began to think
> in English long before I mastered, I won't say the style (I
> haven't done that yet), but the mere uttered speech. . . . You

may take it from me that if I had not known English I wouldn't have written a line for print, in my life.

CONRAD BEGINS A NEW LIFE ON LAND

In November 1894 Conrad met Jessie George, who was twenty-one and pretty. She was not Conrad's intellectual equal, but her disposition complemented Conrad's; her emotional steadiness offset Conrad's moods. From a large working-class family, she had little formal education, but she had worked as a typist and often typed Conrad's manuscripts. Her memoirs describe pleasant times during their year-long courtship that ended when Conrad proposed rather abruptly early in 1896: "Look here, my dear, we had better get married and out of this. Look at the weather. We will get married at once and get over to France. How soon can you be ready? In a week—a fortnight?" His urgency arose not from his passion for her but from his concern about his health and his work and his notion that he would not live long. They were married on March 24, 1896, at the St. George Register Office in London and went immediately to an island off the coast of Brittany in France where Conrad set to work on *The Rescuers*. When the couple returned, they lived at Ivy Walls, Stanford-le-Hope, Essex, in western England. The Conrads had two sons, Borys, born January 15, 1898, and John Alexander, born August 2, 1906.

Besides his devoted wife, Conrad gathered around him a group of loyal and helpful friends. One of his first English friends, G.F.W. Hope, introduced him to Jessie and remained a friend for life; another, Adolf Krieger, often lent Conrad money. Ford Madox Ford, whom Conrad met in 1898, collaborated with Conrad on stories and helped him reconstruct a story that burned accidentally in a fire at his desk. Edward Garnett encouraged Conrad when he doubted his ability to write and published favorable essays on Conrad's work. In one of his most chaotic periods, Conrad found J.B. Pinker, who served as Conrad's agent. He drew up budgets to get Conrad's debts under control and maintained his equanimity when Conrad did not abide by them. Conrad particularly liked John Galsworthy and helped him with his first novel, *Jocelyn*. Galsworthy lent Conrad money and paid his doctor bills and insurance premiums. Conrad often wrote to one or another of these friends when he was sick, broke, depressed, or unable to find his way in a story, and his friends came to his rescue. Collectively, they played a role similar to that of Thaddeus in Conrad's youth.

CONRAD'S EARLY GREAT WORKS

Between 1897 and 1904, Conrad published nine of his most significant works. *The Nigger of the 'Narcissus,'* published in 1897, was a turning point in Conrad's career and his imagination. Frederick Karl explains that he shifted "his concern from Malay subjects to a much deeper and more intense concern with life and death, the mythical sea and the transient individual, survival itself, themes which in ensuing years would become his major subject matter." His next volume, a collection of short stories, *Tales of Unrest,* published in 1898, includes "The Idiots," "Karain," "An Outpost of Progress," "The Return," and "The Lagoon." As was his usual practice, Conrad was working on several stories at the same time. In a letter to Conninghame Graham, Conrad confided that his writing of *Lord Jim* was detained because he was struggling with his philosophy: He saw "no morality, no knowledge and no hope; there is only the consciousness of ourselves which drives us about a world that whether seen in a concave or convex mirror is always a vain and floating experience." Graham responded and Conrad found his way out of his dilemma by creating the narrator Marlow to introduce order. Marlow first appeared in "Youth," a story based on Conrad's experiences on the *Palestine.* With Marlow as narrator, Conrad was able to continue writing *Lord Jim,* and find a balance for his theme, dream versus realism. *Lord Jim,* published in 1900, drew rave reviews; typical was one appearing in the *Manchester Guardian:*

> Mr. Joseph Conrad's work has long been known to novel readers who search for their literature, and to them the publication of *Lord Jim* may rank as a memorable event. It is not to be accepted easily, it cannot be read in a half dose, and by the great public which multiplies editions it may remain neglected or unknown. Yet it is of such remarkable originality and merit that one may look for an emphasis of critical opinion which . . . can force a great reputation in the face of popular apathy or distaste.

During this flurry of writing, he found time to collaborate with Ford Madox Ford on two stories they hoped would reach a wide audience, *The Inheritors,* published in 1901, and *Romance,* published in 1903.

Conrad's next work, *Typhoon,* was published in 1902. The main character, McWhirr, was based on the captain of the *Highland Forest. Typhoon* explores a theme similar to that of *Lord*

Jim, imagination versus pragmatism, only in reverse: Jim has too much imagination, McWhirr too little. *Typhoon* also elicited high praise. It was republished in 1905 as part of a collection, *Typhoon and Other Stories*, which included "Amy Foster," "To-morrow," and "Falk." After the short stories, Conrad again used the narrator Marlow in "Heart of Darkness." The slow trip by river through the dense tropical jungle symbolizes Conrad's complex exploration of evil in the heart of the Congo. First se-rialized in 1899, it was published in a collection, *Youth: A Nar-rative, and Two Other Stories*, in 1902 along with "The End of the Tether," a story based on Conrad's time in Singapore and voyages to Borneo on the *Vidar*.

Conrad worked from December 1902 until August 1904 on his longest, most complex novel, *Nostromo*. Baines de-scribes it as "Conrad's most ambitious feat of imagina-tion. . . . He chose a far larger canvas than he had used be-fore or was to use again; it is as large as that of any great novel except *War and Peace*." *Nostromo* takes place in Costaguana, a fictional country Conrad created from read-ings and from the brief stops he made in South America and the Caribbean while sailing on the *Saint Antoine* in 1876. Its theme is colonialism; according to Jeffrey Meyers in *Joseph Conrad: A Biography*, it addresses three implied questions: "What is the meaning of civilization and progress? What happens when materialism replaces human values? How does colonialism affect traditional societies?" This time the reviews were not good, however, and Conrad was disap-pointed. One critic said the story was too hard to follow and contained too many digressions and irrelevant details, but it "will repay those who give it the close attention it deserves." Reviewers recognized in Conrad's works a new kind of writ-ing. Karl explains that the difference "was, of course, con-nected to Conrad's modernity. 'I am Modern,' he had trum-peted, himself, and that movement away from the Zolaesque social unit toward the less directly ethical, the less explicit, the more purely aesthetic was a measure of this novelty." In short, Conrad's novels focus not on plot and character, nor on social criticism, but on artistic style and inner truth.

TROUBLES AND MISHAPS IN CONRAD'S PERSONAL LIFE

After finishing *Nostromo*, Conrad needed a change and a rest. But first he took Jessie to London in October 1904 for a knee operation to repair damage from an 1889 skating accident that had left her partially crippled, the first of a dozen unsuccessful operations. For thirty years Jessie had trouble walking, and she compensated for her handicap by sitting, eating sweets, reading "trashy" novels, playing dominoes, and gaining weight until obesity made mobility even harder.

Three months after the surgery, the Conrads set off for a vacation on the island of Capri in the Mediterranean, but the trip was anything but relaxing. Conrad had mislaid his favorite eyeglasses and had to leave without them. Jessie forgot part of her false teeth. Since she could barely walk, Jessie had to be carried in chairs. Boarding the ship in Dover, one carrier got his hand stuck between the chair and the gangrail; horrified onlookers feared she would be tipped into the water. In Rome her chair slipped out of a railway carriage, and she was left hanging onto a door. At Naples the sea was too rough for Jessie to travel, so they were held up there for five days. Jessie's nurse got sick, and Conrad caught influenza and bronchitis and could not sleep because of jangled nerves. He wrote to Galsworthy in January:

> The delay of all these days in the hotel has utterly ruined me. . . . The nervous irritation of these days in Naples has prevented me from doing anything. . . . But the whole expedition is a mad thing really, for it rests upon what I am not certain of—my power to produce some sixty thousand words in four months. I feel sick with apprehension at times.

And to Pinker in February:

> I, who now if ever wanted peace to concentrate my thoughts after all the anxieties in London, could not achieve it (as you may guess) in these lodgings. I have worked but badly—there's no use disguising the truth—I've been in a state of exasperation with the eternal something cropping up to distract my mind.

When Conrad was nearly out of the money his friends had provided him for the trip and Pinker had advanced him all that he could, Conrad received news that, by the king's consent, he had been awarded a grant of £500. Relieved, the Conrads went back to England in May.

The trip to Capri characterizes the kind of money troubles, mishaps, and illnesses that plagued the family until near the end of Conrad's life. Conrad spent beyond his income and consistently negotiated for advances on writing he promised to do, a situation that put great strain on his nerves and health and brought on fevers and symptoms of gout. He insisted that he had to get away periodically to relieve the tension of writing, but every trip was a disaster. On a trip to

Montpellier, France, Borys got sick, Conrad's pocket money was stolen, and he started a mattress fire from a lighted cigarette. On a trip to Poland just before World War I, he and Jessie had to hide in a country house to prevent being taken into custody as British citizens until the ambassador could arrange an escape route through Italy. In 1905 Jessie had a nervous breakdown, Borys had scarlet fever, and two months later his skin was burned when the nurse put too much disinfectant in his bathwater. Karl offers an explanation for the chaotic pattern of Conrad's life:

> This accumulation of anxieties, worries, fears, and assorted guilt feelings was connected, evidently, to his way of working and to the functioning of his literary imagination. Apparently, he could not work effectively unless he were close to breakdown, on the edge of psychic disorders, ill in body and mind. Conrad's physical disorders were legion: recurring gout (a hereditary condition), arthritis, delirious fevers, neuralgia, influenza. These, however, were simply the tip. The inner disorder was far greater, and when it was at its most intense, he functioned most effectively artistically.

CONRAD'S LATER WORKS

For fifteen years after the publication of *Nostromo* in 1904, Conrad's life continued much as it had since his marriage. He was sick, he had money problems, he moved to Kent in southeastern England, he enjoyed his old friends and made a few new ones, and he wrote voluminously. Conrad was forty-seven years old in 1904; still to come were eight novels and part of a ninth, six collections of stories and essays, two autobiographical pieces, an essay on politics, and three plays. *The Mirror of the Sea* (1906) is a collection of essays describing episodes from his sailing days. *The Secret Agent* (1907), which had mediocre sales, is a psychological-political detective novel that was adapted as a play. Conrad struggled with *Under Western Eyes* (1911) for more than two years; set in Russia and Switzerland, it tells the story of Razumov, who commits a crime in the first part and confesses and tries to redeem himself in the second. After completing the manuscript in 1910, Conrad suffered a nervous breakdown which required rest and attentive care from Jessie. After his recovery, he wrote *Some Reminiscences*, also called *A Personal Record* (1912), and a collection of stories, *Twixt Land and Sea* (1912), which includes the famous story "The Secret Sharer." *Victory* (1915), also adapted as a play, is a story set in the Malay archipelago about the theme of isolation. Jeffrey Meyers calls *The Shadow-Line* (1917) Conrad's last great work; it is a story based on Conrad's experiences on the *Ortago* sailing from Bangkok to Singapore in 1888. Meyers explains that

> the title of the story refers not only to that twilight region between the naive self-confidence of youth and the more introspective wisdom of maturity, but also to the entrance to the Gulf of Siam, where the former captain was buried and where the ship is mysteriously becalmed off the island of Koh-ring (which also appeared in "The Secret Sharer").

THE WAR YEARS

During World War I, Conrad, now in his late fifties, volunteered to write promotional pieces on Allied plane and ship activities as an observer. His first assignment was an air flight from the Lowestoft Royal Naval Station. In November 1916 he sailed from Granton, near Edinburgh, to repair nets that defended the port from German submarines. He was aboard a twelve-day cruise on the HMS *Ready,* flying under a Norwegian flag and disguised as a merchant ship to entice German subs into a trap. Conrad was exhilarated to be at sea again; his son John said that his father "changed from the gouty invalid I knew to an able and energetic seaman almost as soon as his feet touched the deck." Conrad wrote "Flight," "Well Done!" "Tradition," and "The Unlighted Coast" as a result of these experiences. The war was bad for Conrad's son, however. After Borys failed the exams for entrance to the university, he was commissioned to the Mechanical Transport Corps in 1915, the beginning of a military career. Fighting on the French front a month before Armistice Day, he was gassed and shell-shocked, but recovered after hospitalization. Conrad's worry for his son was coupled with joy when the end of the war brought freedom and independence to his native Poland after 123 years of foreign oppression.

SUCCESS AND FAME

The immediate postwar period brought Conrad financial security and fame. Conrad's popularity really began when Alfred Knopf of Doubleday Publishers in America launched an advertising campaign for *Chance,* marketing it with an attractive cover jacket and catchy chapter titles. The novel sold ten thousand copies. Popularity continued to grow with the publications of *Victory* and *The Shadow-Line. Under Western*

Eyes sold four thousand copies, *The Rover* twenty-six thousand. Between 1914 and 1923 six volumes were published about Conrad: three of criticism, a bibliography, and two memoirs. In 1919 the play adaptation of *Victory* had a successful three-month theatrical run at the Globe in London. Doubleday published a collected edition of Conrad's works.

Conrad's income grew with growing popularity and increased sales, freeing him of debt and at last matching his spending habits. Besides a regular two thousand pounds a year, he received a twelve-thousand-dollar advance on the American collected edition in 1921 and ten thousand pounds on the deluxe English collected edition in 1922. The sale of serial rights for *The Rescue* and film rights for *Victory* earned him another six thousand pounds.

In 1923 Doubleday invited Conrad to America for readings from his works, but fearing his English had too strong a Polish accent, Conrad first practiced on home audiences. Doubleday tried to arrange a quiet entrance into New York Harbor, but pandemonium broke out when Conrad arrived. He wrote to Jessie: "I will not attempt to describe to you my landing because it is indescribable. To be aimed at by forty cameras held by forty men [that looked as if they came out of the slums] is a nerve-shattering experience." Conrad gave a lecture and reading from *Victory* to an audience of two hundred invited guests at the home of railroad magnate Arthur Curtiss James. In his nervousness, Conrad slipped into a heavy Polish accent, but the audience applauded his performance. Of his American trip, he told a friend: "I felt all the time like a man *dans un avion* [in an airplane], in a mist, in a cloud, in a vapour of idealistic phraseology; I was lost, bewildered, amused—but frightened as well."

In addition to his popularity and financial success, Conrad won recognition from the academic community, the prime minister, and fellow artists. He was offered honorary degrees from the universities of Oxford, Cambridge, Edinburgh, Liverpool, and Durham, but declined all, claiming a desire to stay out of the university tradition since he had not finished high school nor attended any university. In May 1924 Prime Minister Ramsey MacDonald sent him an offer of knighthood (Conrad thought the envelope contained his tax bill), but he refused this honor, too. He dreamed of a Nobel Prize, but was never nominated. Painters and sculptors who sought Conrad as a subject have left twenty-six paintings and sketches of him. The most famous artist, Jacob Epstein, sculpted a bust of Conrad. By this time Conrad was too sickly to enjoy his fame. On July 3, 1924, he told a friend: "I feel (and probably look) horribly limp and my spirits stand at about zero. Here you have the horrid truth. But I haven't been well for a long time and *strictly entre nous* [strictly between us] I begin to feel like a cornered rat."

Conrad's death came in August 1924. Friends and his sons had gathered at his home for a holiday weekend on August 1. While taking a friend for a drive, Conrad suffered a mild heart attack and turned back. Doctors came on Saturday and pronounced his condition normal, but Conrad was weak and his breathing heavy. Early on Sunday morning on August 3, Conrad insisted on sitting up in a chair; two hours later he was found dead on the floor. Jessie arranged a Catholic funeral mass on August 7 at St. Thomas Catholic Church in Canterbury. Ironically, his funeral took place at the same time as the Canterbury Cricket Festival, and the town was decorated with banners and filled with tourists. Though Jessie's old leg infirmity prevented her from attending, Conrad's sons and loyal old and new friends gathered at the service, described by Meyers:

> At the graveside in Canterbury cemetery Father Shepherd read the Catholic burial service. "So we left him," Graham wrote, "with his sails all duly furled, ropes flemished down, and with the anchor holding truly in the kind Kentish earth." The moving epigraph from Spenser's *The Faerie Queene*, which Conrad had used on the title page of *The Rover*, was cut into the grey granite:

> Sleep after toyle, port after stormie seas,
> Ease after warre, death after life, does greatly please.

CHAPTER 1

Conrad's Themes and Methods

READINGS ON
JOSEPH CONRAD

The Prose Writer's Goals and Methods

Joseph Conrad

In his preface to *The Nigger of the 'Narcissus,'* Conrad explains the purpose of the prose writer's art: to capture the work and actions of individuals in a way that conveys a glimpse into the truth of life. The artist appeals to the reader by stirring the emotions that lie invisibly beneath the surface.

A work that aspires, however humbly, to the condition of art should carry its justification in every line. And art itself may be defined as a single-minded attempt to render the highest kind of justice to the visible universe, by bringing to light the truth, manifold and one, underlying its every aspect. It is an attempt to find in its forms, in its colours, in its light, in its shadows, in the aspects of matter and in the facts of life what of each is fundamental, what is enduring and essential— their one illuminating and convincing quality—the very truth of their existence. The artist, then, like the thinker or the scientist, seeks the truth and makes his appeal. Impressed by the aspect of the world the thinker plunges into ideas, the scientist into facts—whence, presently, emerging they make their appeal to those qualities of our being that fit us best for the hazardous enterprise of living. They speak authoritatively to our common-sense, to our intelligence, to our desire of peace or to our desire of unrest; not seldom to our prejudices, sometimes to our fears, often to our egoism—but always to our credulity. And their words are heard with reverence, for their concern is with weighty matters: with the cultivation of our minds and the proper care of our bodies, with the attainment of our ambitions, with the perfection of the means and the glorification of our precious aims.

It is otherwise with the artist.

Joseph Conrad, preface to the original (1897) edition of *The Nigger of the "Narcissus."*

ART APPEALS TO THE EMOTIONS

Confronted by the same enigmatical[1] spectacle the artist descends within himself, and in that lonely region of stress and strife, if he be deserving and fortunate, he finds the terms of his appeal. His appeal is made to our less obvious capacities: to that part of our nature which, because of the warlike conditions of existence, is necessarily kept out of sight within the more resisting and hard qualities—like the vulnerable body within a steel armour. His appeal is less loud, more profound, less distinct, more stirring—and sooner forgotten. Yet its effect endures forever. The changing wisdom of successive generations discards ideas, questions facts, demolishes theories. But the artist appeals to that part of our being which is not dependent on wisdom: to that in us which is a gift and not an acquisition—and, therefore, more permanently enduring. He speaks to our capacity for delight and wonder, to the sense of mystery surrounding our lives, to our sense of pity, and beauty, and pain; to the latent feeling of fellowship with all creation—and to the subtle but invincible conviction of solidarity that knits together the loneliness of innumerable hearts, to the solidarity in dreams, in joy, in sorrow, in aspirations, in illusions, in hope, in fear, which binds men to each other, which binds together all humanity—the dead to the living and the living to the unborn.

It is only some such train of thought, or rather of feeling, that can in a measure explain the aim of the attempt, made in the tale which follows, to present an unrestful episode in the obscure lives of a few individuals out of all the disregarded multitude of the bewildered, the simple and the voiceless. For, if any part of truth dwells in the belief confessed above, it becomes evident that there is not a place of splendour or a dark corner of the earth that does not deserve, if only a passing glance of wonder and pity. The motive then, may be held to justify the matter of the work; but this preface, which is simply an avowal of endeavour, cannot end here—for the avowal is not yet complete.

FICTION APPEALS TO TEMPERAMENT

Fiction—if it at all aspires to be art—appeals to temperament. And in truth it must be, like painting, like music, like

1. difficult to understand or explain

all art, the appeal of one temperament to all the other innumerable temperaments whose subtle and resistless power endows passing events with their true meaning, and creates the moral, the emotional atmosphere of the place and time. Such an appeal to be effective must be an impression conveyed through the senses; and, in fact, it cannot be made in any other way, because temperament, whether individual or collective, is not amenable to persuasion. All art, therefore, appeals primarily to the senses, and the artistic aim when expressing itself in written words must also make its appeal through the senses, if its high desire is to reach the secret spring of responsive emotions. It must strenuously aspire to the plasticity of sculpture, to the colour of painting, and to the magic suggestiveness of music—which is the art of arts. And it is only through complete, unswerving devotion to the perfect blending of form and substance; it is only through an unremitting never-discouraged care for the shape and ring of sentences that an approach can be made to plasticity, to colour, and that the light of magic suggestiveness may be brought to play for an evanescent instant over the commonplace surface of words: of the old, old words, worn thin, defaced by ages of careless usage.

MAKING A READER *SEE* A MOMENT

The sincere endeavour to accomplish that creative task, to go as far on that road as his strength will carry him, to go undeterred by faltering, weariness or reproach, is the only valid justification for the worker in prose. And if his conscience is clear, his answer to those who in the fulness of a wisdom which looks for immediate profit, demand specifically to be edified, consoled, amused; who demand to be promptly improved, or encouraged, or frightened, or shocked, or charmed, must run thus:—My task which I am trying to achieve is, by the power of the written word to make you hear, to make you feel—it is, before all, to make you *see*. That—and no more, and it is everything. If I succeed, you shall find there according to your deserts: encouragement, consolation, fear, charm—all you demand—and, perhaps, also that glimpse of truth for which you have forgotten to ask.

To snatch in a moment of courage, from the remorseless rush of time, a passing phase of life, is only the beginning of the task. The task approached in tenderness and faith is to hold up unquestioningly, without choice and without fear, the rescued fragment before all eyes in the light of a sincere mood. It is to show its vibration, its colour, its form; and through its movement, its form, and its colour, reveal the substance of its truth—disclose its inspiring secret: the stress and passion within the core of each convincing moment. In a single-minded attempt of that kind, if one be deserving and fortunate, one may perchance attain to such clearness of sincerity that at last the presented vision of regret or pity, of terror or mirth, shall awaken in the hearts of the beholders that feeling of unavoidable solidarity; of the solidarity in mysterious origin, in toil, in joy, in hope, in uncertain fate, which binds men to each other and all mankind to the visible world

A MOMENT CAUGHT OFFERS A GLIMPSE OF TRUTH

It is evident that he who, rightly or wrongly, holds by the convictions expressed above cannot be faithful to any one of the temporary formulas of his craft. The enduring part of them—the truth which each only imperfectly veils—should abide with him as the most precious of his possessions, but they all: Realism, Romanticism, Naturalism, even the unofficial sentimentalism (which like the poor, is exceedingly difficult to get rid of), all these gods must, after a short period of fellowship, abandon him—even on the very threshold of the temple—to the stammerings of his conscience and to the outspoken consciousness of the difficulties of his work. In that uneasy solitude the supreme cry of Art for Art itself, loses the exciting ring of its apparent immorality. It sounds far off. It has ceased to be a cry, and is heard only as a whisper, often incomprehensible, but at times and faintly encouraging.

Sometimes, stretched at ease in the shade of a roadside tree, we watch the motions of a labourer in a distant field, and after a time, begin to wonder languidly as to what the fellow may be at. We watch the movement of his body, the waving of his arms, we see him bend down, stand up, hesitate, begin again. It may add to the charm of an idle hour to be told the purpose of his exertions. If we know he is trying to lift a stone, to dig a ditch, to uproot a stump, we look with a more real interest at his efforts; we are disposed to condone the jar of his agitation upon the restfulness of the landscape; and even, if in a brotherly frame of mind, we may bring ourselves to forgive his failure. We understood his object, and, after all, the fellow has tried, and perhaps he had not the strength—and perhaps he had not the knowledge. We forgive, go on our way—and forget.

And so it is with the workman of art. Art is long and life is short, and success is very far off. And thus, doubtful of strength to travel so far, we talk a little about the aim—the aim of art, which, like life itself, is inspiring, difficult—obscured by mists. It is not in the clear logic of a triumphant conclusion; it is not in the unveiling of one of those heartless secrets which are called the Laws of Nature. It is not less great, but only more difficult.

To arrest, for the space of a breath, the hands busy about the work of the earth, and compel men entranced by the sight of distant goals to glance for a moment at the surrounding vision of form and colour, of sunshine and shadows; to make them pause for a look, for a sigh, for a smile—such is the aim, difficult and evanescent,[2] and reserved only for a very few to achieve. But sometimes, by the deserving and the fortunate, even that task is accomplished. And when it is accomplished—behold!—all the truth of life is there: a moment of vision, a sigh, a smile—and the return to an eternal rest.

2. quick to vanish

Conrad Learns His Craft

Walter F. Wright

Walter F. Wright explains the zeal with which Conrad, a native of Poland and a seaman by trade, pursued the art of writing stories and novels. Conrad studied other writers, Wright says, for their views of the world and for their technique. Through discipline and imagination, Conrad learned to transform his personal experiences into fiction. Wright explains that Conrad was determined to write in English because in English he found an abundantly fresh, concrete vocabulary. Walter F. Wright has taught at North Dakota State University, Washington State University, and the University of Nebraska. He is the author of six books of criticism, including *Romance and Tragedy in Joseph Conrad* and books on George Meredith, Henry James, and Thomas Hardy.

Whatever Joseph Conrad wrote, whether fiction, criticism, or general observations on life, reveals in its imagery and rhythms the passionate dramatic intensity with which he pursued his art. His tone ranges from the bitterness of revulsion, when he sometimes mocks a story that has been exhausting his nervous energy for weeks, to a nearly ecstatic reminiscence of the adventures of composition. His philosophic commentaries are equally diverse—at times railing at human folly, as in certain letters to Cunninghame Graham,[1] and, at others, stressing the mystic nature of human solidarity. Both extremes—even like those which confront Marlow in *Heart of Darkness*—were for Conrad the very stuff of reality.

It was with reality that the writer of fiction must, of course, begin; and reality was not something that he could

---

1. Scottish politician Robert Cunninghame Graham was also known as the widely traveled author of adventurous tales.

find awaiting his factual recording. Quite the contrary. It had to be created by the disciplined imagination. Underlying every sentence in Conrad's literary criticism is a principle stated explicitly in "Books": "In truth every novelist must begin by creating for himself a world, great or little, in which he can honestly believe." Such a world Conrad found in the sea adventures of Cooper's Long Tom and the psychological ordeal of James's Fleda Vetch, in the ingenuous sketches of Daudet and the artful studies of Turgenev and Proust.

CONRAD'S STUDY OF OTHER WRITERS

Indeed, Conrad's interests in fiction were wide ranging. Though naturally annoyed to find himself called a "spinner of sea-yarns," he could view life as a romance of adventure, a revelation, as in *Typhoon*, of the genius of the human adaptation to the forces of nature, and he could look upon nature itself as "spectacle." If such writers as Cooper or Marryat did not press the symbolism of their incidents, Conrad could still value their writing for its testing of the courage and ingenuity of the human mind. He respected, too, the social novels of Galsworthy and the attempts by Arnold Bennett to catch the tone and color of the five towns and of London. He admitted obliquely to the influence of Maupassant, whose unadorned, unflinching representation of life's tragic hardness he found both honest and artistically meaningful. Two major writers came in for his condemnation. Tolstoi he accused of sentimentality and of using Christianity as a solution to human problems. Though there are incidents in his own novels that are in accord with Christian beliefs, Conrad was distrustful of the Christian perspective for surveying man's relation to the Universe and even to his fellow men. His strongest censure was for Dostoevski, whom he attacked for "prehistoric mouthings." Ironically, he has sometimes been compared with Dostoevski, since both dealt with inner compulsions, impulses not understood by their heroes, and since the search for atonement in such a story as *Under Western Eyes* recalls that in *Crime and Punishment*. Though he did not expand his violent outbursts against the Russian novelist, Conrad appears to have felt that Dostoevski floundered in sentimentality instead of maintaining artistic restraint. Of his feelings for the Classics and for Shakespeare we have occasional reverential hints. He speaks with pride of his father's translating of Shakespeare, and in *The Mirror of the Sea* he suggests analogy of events with those in the classical epics. Reality was always for Conrad a romance of adventure, potentially of epic proportions; it was most often a tragic one.

For some of the authors whom Conrad admired literary composition was not unduly strenuous; or at least they did not lament its exactions. For Conrad himself it represented nervous fatigue or indeed agony. Yet it was the one great adventure, better even than that offered by ships and the sea because it was all-inclusive. He renounced the life of master mariner, in which he had achieved some competence, because he could not resist the lure of a perilous art at which he was but a novice. Writing of Henry James, who had spent years perfecting his craft, he spoke accurately for both James and himself: "The artist in his calling of interpreter creates . . . because he must. He is so much of a voice that, for him, silence is like death. . . ." Allowing for the nostalgia of the successful practitioner as he looks back on the hazards he has passed, one nevertheless senses in *A Personal Record* the spell under which Conrad performed his toil. Repeatedly in his short stories and novels he demonstrated that the only reward worth having was a "perfect love of the work." Such a love took possession of a sailor—or an author—without his conscious awareness, and yet it blessed only those who deliberately accepted the rigors of their trade and its eternal threat of tragedy. In *A Personal Record* Conrad compared the tribulations of writing to the "westward winter passage round Cape Horn." Each amounted to a "lonely struggle under a sense of over-matched littleness, for no reward that could be adequate, but for the mere winning of a longitude." The nature of the adventure itself was an important subject for criticism.

A NOVELIST CREATES REALITY

The task of the novelist being the creation of reality, he had to seek hints of truth in his own experience. His works would always be spiritually autobiographic in that, as author, he could be the "figure behind the veil." In his Author's Note to *Typhoon* Conrad spoke of "a conscientious regard for the truth of my own sensations," and, again, in that to *Within the Tides*, of "the obligation of a more scrupulous fidelity to the truth of my own sensations." Besides the Author's Notes and *A Personal Record*, a number of the letters discuss the transformation that occurred as an event or person from the world of actuality became the touchstone for an incident or a characterization in Conrad's fiction. Most notable, of course, was Almayer. The hero of *Almayer's Folly* is not the man whom the novelist saw in the flesh, and yet Conrad's sensations as he contemplated the tragic derelict gave him his assurance that his novel was not untrue. Indeed, in various Author's Notes and in *A Personal Record* Conrad begins his discussion of a story as a work of art by alluding to its origin in historical fact. Whereas Thomas Hardy, however, sometimes justified inferior poems by saying that their narrated incidents actually happened, Conrad, on the contrary, was always the artist. The incident, for him, had happened, but so had countless others. His point was that he had recognized in it or in a person—even as Henry James did in the "germs" of his stories—an artistic significance. Having made his discovery, he had something valid with which to work. What finally developed was a creation of the artist's imagination.

Inasmuch as the writer of fiction was always present, even though behind the veil, there was inevitably a subjective aspect to his created world. "This world," Conrad remarked in "Books," "cannot be made otherwise than in his own image; it is fated to remain individual and a little mysterious. . . ." Nevertheless, the author could confidently expect to touch cords in the hearts of others; for, even while admitting the individuality of the novelist's world, Conrad continued, ". . . yet it must resemble something already familiar to the experience, the thoughts and the sensations of his readers." And in the Preface to *The Nigger of the "Narcissus"* he had previously written of the author's responsibility to his reader: "My task which I am trying to achieve is, by the power of the written word to make you hear, to make you feel—it is, before all, to make you see."

CREATING REALITY WITH CONCRETE IMAGERY, METAPHOR, AND SYMBOL

To make others see, the author himself must first see distinctly and render objectively. Despite the inevitable subjectivity which would give the tone to his art, he must be preoccupied with the concrete substance of his story and search always for the precise, individualizing detail. In several letters Conrad gives instruction in the simple, yet difficult, elements

of composition. In each instance he would have his corre-
spondents—Clifford, Galsworthy, Mrs. Sanderson, and others—recast lines that are imprecise and essentially sentimental because they assert rather than exhibit the essence of a
scene. He does not correct the passages by applying mechanical rules. Instead, he attacks the problem at its beginning by
visualizing the actions which the authors themselves have
not adequately seen. In short, with his own sense of life to
guide him, he looked always for the concrete, objective
images which moved him and which, given the solidarity of
mankind, should kindle a sympathetic response in a sensitive
reader.

The writer must, of course, employ metaphor and symbol if
his fictitious persons and incidents were to have universal
implication. In his very first work Conrad struggled, at times
tediously, to develop the symbolic importance of his scenes, but
by 1900 he had learned how to convey it obliquely; and though
his metaphors continued occasionally to be florid, he generally thereafter evoked rather than asserted the implications of his
scenes. In *The Mirror of the Sea, A Personal Record,* and the
Author's Notes the symbolic nature of art is taken for granted.
It is through art as symbol that communication with a reader
takes place, for it thus becomes a touchstone for the reader's
creative interpretation of his own spiritual experience.

CONRAD'S PREFERENCE FOR THE ENGLISH LANGUAGE

"Give me the right word and the right accent and I will move
the world"—in this famous pronouncement Conrad used the
morally neutral right word *move*, as the power of rhetoric
could be for ill as well as good, though he, of course, hoped
that his own words and accent would make for the world's
enlightenment. And for his purposes he chose the English
language. Although Ford Madox Ford[2] reported that sometimes, in searching for an apt phrase, he and Conrad would
come up with a French term, Conrad explicitly stated that
there was no accident in his determining to write in English.
What he does not say anywhere, but what is implicit in his
fiction is that he always had a feeling for the etymology of
English words and that common metaphors had for him a
freshness stemming from their newness. The language was,
in short, vividly concrete.

2. with whom Conrad wrote *The Inheritors* (1901)

Often in a single letter or essay we find Conrad talking about the philosophic questions that relate literature to life, his own mental habits as a novelist, and the craft of literary composition. For a moment the focus is on one of the three, but they are finally inseparable. In discussing the genius of other novelists he was usually more detached than when speaking of himself; but he was still engaged in a romance of discovery, and the tone of his critical essays conveys the excitement of exploration. Indeed, he may be said to have defined his own role as critic in the words he quoted from Anatole France: "The good critic is he who relates the adventures of his soul among masterpieces."

Major Elements in Conrad's Stories

Jerry Allen

Jerry Allen outlines common elements in seven of
Conrad's short works. Allen explains that Conrad drew
on his sea experiences for vivid settings (the East) and
character types (the alienated outsider), and she identifies Conrad's common themes: the failure to live up
to personal ideals, the basic similarity of all humans
regardless of geography or race, and the inner isolation of all individuals. Briefly, Allen touches on
Conrad's "ambling" method of storytelling and the
poetry of Conrad's sentences. Jerry Allen was a journalist for the *New York-Herald Tribune* and the
National Broadcasting Company. She is the author of
biographies of Mark Twain and Joseph Conrad, the
latter entitled *Sunshine: Biography of Joseph Conrad*
and *The Sea Years of Joseph Conrad.*

Joseph Conrad, one of the very great masters of the novel (his
short stories show an almost equal gift), had the rare distinc-
tion of being recognized as an English classic in his own lifetime. He died in England on August 3, 1924, in his rented
house, Oswalds, at Bishopsbourne in Kent. Such is the time-
lessness of the subjects he deals with—his penetrating study
of the alienated, the outsider, to mention only one—that he
seems to us contemporary. As an artist he is an "original."
He fits into no category adequately except that of "ancestor"
of much of modern fiction, for he fathered the psychological
novel, the political novel, and the intellectual mystery story
as we know them today. There was in Conrad, said H.L.
Mencken, "something almost suggesting the vastness of a
natural phenomenon."

A man with an extraordinary mind, Conrad led an equally extraordinary life. It enabled him to write authoritatively

Excerpted from Jerry Allen, introduction to *Great Short Works of Joseph Conrad,* by
Joseph Conrad. Introduction and bibliography copyright © 1966, 1967 by Harper &
Row, Publishers, Inc. Reprinted by permission of HarperCollins Publishers, Inc.

of human problems in a wide range, to place his stories in settings that literally cover the globe. The realism of his fiction and the geographical scope of it owe much to the fact that he wrote of what he saw, what he knew. His fiction grew out of his life, and his life in itself was a drama. . . .

SEA EXPERIENCES AS SOURCE FOR STORIES

For twenty years, from 1874 to 1894, he was a seaman on French and British ships. For the major part of those years he served in the British merchant marine, rising rapidly from ordinary seaman to captain, in command of a ship at thirty. His sea life gave Conrad the wealth of dramatic material he was to draw upon for his writing and also the name he is known by. British seamen mangled the unfamiliar Polish name of Korzeniowski (it appears in the sea documents of his time in such distorted forms as "Konkorzentowski"), and before he left the sea he had reduced his name to Joseph Conrad. He had also, at twenty-eight, become a naturalized British subject. . . .

He had survived hurricanes and gales at sea in an era when such fragile wind-driven craft as those on which he sailed were lost in large numbers each day; and he had survived two shipwrecks.

One of the shipwrecks is related in "Youth." This story which Conrad wrote when he was forty and called "a feat of memory," is factually true. It is the magnificent narrative of the ill-fated voyage of the coal carrier *Palestine* (the *Judea* in "Youth") on which Conrad served as second mate. Nearing the end of her voyage from England to Bangkok she blew up in Bangka Strait, off Sumatra. Though injured in the explosion, Conrad, then twenty-five, made his way in a small boat to the nearest shore and at Muntok on Bangka Island had his first view of the East—"the East of the ancient navigators, so old, so mysterious, resplendent and sombre, living and unchanged, full of danger and promise."

The East figures prominently in Conrad's work. His first novel, *Almayer's Folly*, is based on the village of Berau in Borneo and the people he knew there when he served as chief mate of the *Vidar*, and "The Lagoon" stems from that Borneo time and place. It is the second short story Conrad ever wrote, composed after the completion of two novels. Vivid as to setting, compassionate in mood, its theme—that of a courageous and normally reliable man who fails in a moment of crisis—is one he comes back to often.

His contact with Borneo—in a sense his "literary birth-place," for, from his first novel almost to his last, he repeatedly returned to that setting—came two-thirds of the way along in his sea career. After Borneo he secured his first command, the barque *Otago,* becoming master of her in Bangkok. Nearly twenty-five years later he was to draw upon that initial voyage down the Gulf of Siam for the background of "The Secret Sharer." This brilliant story of man's dual nature (the obvious self, the hidden self) is a keystone in Conrad's work.

Conrad was just under thirty-two when he began his first novel, *Almayer's Folly,* in London in 1889. With only a small part of it written, he made up his mind, on an impulse, to go to Africa, to the Congo, a part of the world he had never seen. The interior of that vast territory of supposed but unknown mineral wealth, privately owned by King Leopold II of Belgium, was unexplored country. Assigned to the command of a river steamer scheduled to transport an exploring expedition, Conrad arrived in the Congo in 1890. In that year European exploitation of the Africans was at a gruesome height; slaves, captured by Arab raiders, were still being shipped abroad. "Heart of Darkness," directly autobiographical, carries the full force of Conrad's reaction to the bitter six months he spent in the Congo. . . .

In 1894 his career as a seaman ended. The following year, with the publication of *Almayer's Folly,* his career as a writer began. He was thirty-seven. During the following thirty years, living in England but making short stays on the Continent, the twenty-seven volumes of his work were produced. . . .

Much has been made of the fact that he was able to write so brilliantly in English—he is one of the very greatest of English stylists—when this was a language he did not begin to use until he was twenty. But in fact he was a gifted linguist. He knew French and Polish equally well, having learned them as a child, and speedily acquiring fluency in English on British ships, he was also to learn Malay quickly when the need for that arose.

The poetry of his style has in it something of the rise and fall, the cadence of the sea. "There was hate in the way she was handled, and a ferocity in the blows that fell"; "a burst and turmoil of sparks that seemed to fill with flying fire the night patient and watchful, the vast night lying silent upon the sea"; "Black shapes crouched, lay, sat, between the trees, leaning against the trunks, clinging to the earth, half coming out, half effaced within the dim light, in all the attitudes of pain, abandonment, and despair"—in such passages as these, typical of Conrad's sonorous style, there is an echo of the sea's majestic rhythm. . . .

CONRAD CONCERNED WITH "IDEAL VALUE"

Much as he used the life he knew best, that of the sea, for the stage of his fiction—as Hardy used the heath and Dickens the city—the core of Conrad's concern is with what he called "the ideal value of things, events, and people." A sentence in "The Secret Sharer" gives a clue to his meaning of "ideal value" and it is this one: "I wondered how far I should turn out faithful to that ideal conception of one's own personality every man sets up for himself secretly." In our private dreams—and who does not have them?—we see ourselves acting in a manner verging on the heroic. But some unlucky mischance, some unendurable strain, can play havoc with those ideals of behavior. Through fear, passionate love or an equally passionate hate, the crushing stress of crisis—through any one of a variety of pressures, judgment can be dissolved. In that conflict of reason versus emotion, the climax Conrad defines as "the point of honor and the point of passion," the ideal self is lost, if only for a vital instant. Such a self-failure happens to Leggatt in "The Secret Sharer." In "Heart of Darkness," the moral and symbolic drama recognized as a masterpiece of English literature, the failure of Kurtz is total, his disintegration complete. Kurtz personifies the evil latent in man, the demonic force circumstances can unleash. On another level he symbolizes the failure of the white man in his dealings with the dark-skinned races of the world. Offering insights into the Congo of today, into the very issue of race, "Heart of Darkness" has a special timeliness.

Bigotry outraged Conrad—a response rather rare in his Victorian times—and two of the stories here illustrate a view he held: that men—regardless of race or color or creed, or even of locality—are basically alike, exhibiting many of the same virtues and flaws. In "Heart of Darkness" the non-hero is an educated European, a white man who in the largest sense betrays his brothers, all mankind. In "The Lagoon" the non-hero, Arsat, betrays the brother he loves; Arsat is a

Malay. Elsewhere in his fiction Conrad allocates virtues to characters with the same lack of bias.

THE THEME OF INNER ISOLATION

Among his many themes one stands out. "We live, as we dream—alone. . . ." Marlow's words in "Heart of Darkness" summarize the inner isolation, the apartness each of us knows. It is inherent in, to use the now-so-popular phrase, the human condition. Since being an individual is a lonely state and an exposed one, man has ever sought to break out of it by joining the group, becoming "one of us." But the payment required for that joining, that acceptance, is conformity. The nonconformist may be, and often is, rejected by society—for a point of view or a way of life differing from the norm in any given place, for faults unlucky accidents reveal, for mistakes, for crimes, even for the failure to be well born in a climate where that matters. Conrad would wish for a world of brotherhood (he gives such a one in "Youth"), for a harmonious world where integrity, loyalty, and honor are the virtues supreme, but it is the outsider who has his sympathy. Perhaps because he knew the role so well himself. An orphan, always the only Pole on British ships, a Shakespeare-reading youth with the dress of a dandy, he was an anomaly in the roustabout world of seamen. At a time when education and jobs were scarce, the men who shared the forecastle with him were frequently illiterate.

On board sailing ships, where jeopardy came with little warning, the action of each man at such a time could affect his own survival and that of his fellows. This repeated state of crisis was normal at sea, and some inevitably failed that testing. "Do you know what *you* would have done? Do you?" is a question Conrad poses in *Lord Jim*, and throughout his work it is a question subtly asked. For he is concerned with truth, "the stress and passion within the core of each convincing moment," and his goal is, in his own words, "to make you *see*." He looks at the world as it actually is and, with compassion for those struggling with "how to be," portrays the fractionalizations and the injustices he finds.

CONRAD'S UNUSUAL TALES AND REAL CHARACTERS

Aware that no single position offers a grandstand view of truth, he uses an ambling method in his storytelling, circling a situation, flashing a variety of glimpses as he passes. Or again, as in the stories here, he approaches a human problem from opposite directions. "Youth" is the story of men knit together by a crisis; *The Nigger of the* Narcissus tells of men sundered by it. "Typhoon" is the story of a stormy voyage presented as comedy; *The Nigger of the* Narcissus is again a stormy voyage, this time tragedy.

Conrad's third novel, *The Nigger of the* Narcissus, was his first tale of the sea. It was inspired by two shipboard deaths, one occurring on the *Narcissus* when he was second mate, the other when he served in the same capacity on board the *Tilkhurst.* Of this novel Conrad wrote, "It is the book by which, not as a novelist perhaps, but as an artist striving for the utmost sincerity of expression, I am willing to stand or fall." As a piece of storytelling it is a flawless gem. As a study of group psychology it has few, if any, equals. As a parable it is the round of life condensed into a single voyage: the casual beginning, the coming together; the storms that nature (or life) presents, the dissensions that man in his fear creates; survival, the safe landing, with sunshine falling "on the anxious faces of forgetful men."

[In the 1920s] the characters in Conrad's work were described as "not only beyond comparison the most striking, the most original, the most fascinating, but the most romantic, in the whole of contemporary fiction." Few today would disagree, even expanding the time down to the present, with any but the "romantic" part of that judgment. New facts were made known in the biography *The Sea Years of Joseph Conrad*, and these dramatic discoveries go far to explain why Conrad's characters have the vitality they do. They are not romantic inventions as was earlier assumed; they were drawn from life. The original of Lord Jim was a Singapore ship's officer named Augustine Podmore Williams who, like Jim, was involved in a famous sea case; Tom Lingard, the heroic figure in three of Conrad's novels, was based upon another actual man, Captain William Lingard; Kurtz in "Heart of Darkness" owes his fictional existence to an Englishman in the Congo, Major Edmund Musgrave Barttelot; Jimmy, Donkin and Belfast of *The Nigger of the* Narcissus were among the many in that novel modelled upon seamen with whom Conrad sailed. . . .

Authors [in the second half of the twentieth century] are more often found to be "like Conrad" than "like" anyone else. He is a reference point in discussions of eloquent style ("in the still night bats flitted in and out of the boughs like fluttering flakes of denser darkness"); he is the measuring name for psychological novels, for realistic characterization. Or for fiction, appearing offhand as straightforward and stirring enough as that, yet having beneath its convincing surface layers of serious thought presented symbolically, creating the challenge of what a story "means."

Another Conradian trait (the adjective itself now so much in literary usage is recognition of his originator's role) is the atmospheric depth of settings, of backgrounds that, far from being dormant stage sets, are vital to the narrative's illusion. The jungle stillness of "The Lagoon" is an actor in that story, as is the wild sea in *The Nigger of the* Narcissus.

Conrad's storytelling is a very intricate art, but his method might be said to take two forms, the direct or more simple relation and the complex story replete with subterranean meanings. Pairs of these appear here: "Typhoon" (simple) and *The Nigger of the* Narcissus (complex); "An Outpost of Progress" (simple) and "Heart of Darkness" (complex); "Youth" (simple) and "The Secret Sharer" (complex). "The Lagoon," a love story, stands midway.

To some extent "The Lagoon" harkens back to *Romeo and Juliet.* Here Malay lovers in an Eastern island kingdom defy their ruler, Si Dendring, and the woman, Inchi Midah, who forbid their romance. They escape by canoe and in the course of their flight their protector, Arsat's brother, is killed. It is Arsat's guilt—saving Diamelen, the girl he loves, at the cost of the brother he also loves—that foreshadows the theme of divided loyalties developed in Conrad's later work.

CONRAD'S BELIEF THAT ALL HUMANS SHARE COMMON EXPERIENCES

The viewpoint which set Conrad so much apart in his own day and draws him so near to ours is reflected in these seven stories. "I am content to sympathize with common mortals," he stated it, "no matter where they live; in houses or in tents, in the streets under a fog, or in the forest behind the dark line of dismal mangroves that fringe the vast solitude of the sea." His people of the East and of Africa, his seamen, are common mortals all. "There is a bond between us and that humanity so far away," he told his American and European readers. "Their hearts—like ours—must endure . . . the curse of facts and the blessing of illusions."

Untouched by the "blessing of illusions" are the unimaginative, down-to-earth men like Captain MacWhirr in "Typhoon." To him "books are only good to muddle your head and make you jumpy." Any problem is "plain and straight." Never troubled by introspection and so immune to fear, he dismisses the typhoon with "It will be bad, and there's an end." This storm-piece brilliantly succeeds as a drama at sea. As its second purpose it portrays human reactions in a time of crisis, through the contrasting characters of Jukes and Captain MacWhirr.

In the same mold as Captain MacWhirr are Kayerts and Carlier in "An Outpost of Progress," a story consistently holding the irony of the title. As agents of the Great Trading Company set down in an African outpost to collect ivory, these two "perfectly insignificant and incapable individuals" disintegrate rapidly when detached from their familiar surroundings and routines. As the storm brings on the crisis in "Typhoon," here it is the opposite or negative force, the insidious drain of isolation. This story with its fierce statement on human exploitation reflected Conrad's stay in the Congo. "All the bitterness of those days, all my puzzled wonder as to the meaning of all I saw—all my indignation at masquerading philanthropy have been with me again while I wrote." Written very early (1896) in his career and falling short of the quality of his best work, it is significant as a first step toward that powerful inward journey, the soul-searching "Heart of Darkness.". . .

As only great stories do, they offer in abundance "encouragement, consolation, fear, charm—all you demand—and, perhaps, also that glimpse of truth for which you have forgotten to ask."

Conrad as Painter

Adam Gillon

Adam Gillon argues that Conrad's prose is imitative of painting, citing passages in which Conrad's descriptions are particularly vivid. Though Conrad's novels have many examples of painterly techniques, Gillon focuses on *Lord Jim* and analyzes the way Conrad creates a portrait of Jim in stages, from a broad outline to inner detail. Adam Gillon has taught English and comparative literature at the State University of New York at New Paltz and served as president of the Joseph Conrad Society of America. He is the author of *The Eternal Solitary: A Study of Joseph Conrad.*

Arthur Symons, a poet whose work Conrad read and admired, wrote a moving tribute after the novelist's death. He likened Conrad's "look into the darkness at the end of the long avenue" to that of Shakespeare, Balzac, and Rodin, thus explaining the nature of his appeal as an artist: "Only great painters have created atmosphere to the extent that Conrad has: and Conrad's is if anything more mysterious, menacing and more troubling to the senses and to the nerves, than theirs; he creates thrilling effects by mere force of suggestion, elusive as some vague mist, full of illusion, of rare magic, which can become poisonous or sorcerous."

Indeed, it is quite easy to draw an analogy between Conrad's art and painting, especially because the visual image is one of the most basic grounds between the novel and painting. And Conrad, from the very first, was concerned with images. In 1899, he wrote to Cunninghame Graham, referring to *Heart of Darkness:* "I don't start with an abstract notion. I start with *definite images* and as their rendering is true some little effect is produced.". . . He reaffirmed this point in a letter to H.G. Wells in 1905: "But since, O Brother!, I am a novelist I must speak in *images.*" When Conrad penned his celebrated Preface to *The Nigger of the*

From *Joseph Conrad: Comparative Essays* by Adam Gillon, edited by Raymond Brebach, Texas Tech University Press, copyright © 1994. Reprinted with permission of the publisher and the author.

"Narcissus," he singled out the visual as being the most important element of his craft: "My task which I am trying to achieve is, by the power of the written word to make you hear, to make you feel—it is, before all, to make you *see.* That—and no more, and it is everything.". . .

There is no doubt, thus, among the critics of ample grounds for an analogy between the visual arts and Conrad's imagery. To what extent, however, does Conrad himself consider fiction as being analogous to painting? Or to the eye of the camera? In what sense can his representations of people, nature, and things inanimate be seen as verbal paintings, snapshots, or the moving pictures of a roving camera?

Indeed, painting was one of the arts Conrad had in mind when stating his artistic credo, in that same Preface to *The Nigger:* "Fiction—if it at all aspires to be art—appeals to temperament. And in truth it must be *like painting,* like music, like all art. . . . Such an appeal to be effective must be *an impression* conveyed through the senses . . . it must strenuously aspire to the plasticity of sculpture, to *the colour of painting,* and to the magic suggestiveness of music—which is the art of arts.". . .

As Dr. Bernard C. Meyer pointed out, despite Conrad's intense dislike of being photographed, "he evidently had no aversion to making pictures of others. . . . He either made or copied a number of sketches of women." . . . The drawings show Conrad as a fairly competent draftsman who can attain a likeness of a face with a few strokes of his pen or chalk. . . . He also knows how to exaggerate some parts of the human anatomy (thighs, waist, hair, hands) in order to achieve a comic, satiric, or dramatic effect. Whatever symbolic meaning can be read into these drawings, it is clear that Conrad could draw and that he looked at people and things with the eyes of a visual artist, cognizant of the technical task, which, of course, is to make the spectator *see* what the artist has perceived. . . .

CONRAD'S USE OF PAINTERS' TECHNIQUES

In most of his works Conrad selects a principal color scheme, often a dramatic contrast between the dark and the light, or focuses our vision upon a dominant image: a snake-like river in the Congo; white ivory; black, impenetrable forests; the immaculately white form of Jim; the shining silver buttons of Nostromo's uniform; or the shining silver ingots. Even some of his nonvisual descriptions of character reinforce the "color scheme" of the intended portrait or draw our attention to the artist's design. Thus, the often excessive use of appositional phrases no less than his adjectival style in descriptions of scenery produces the result achieved by the painter with a bold stroke of his brush or chalk. . . .

In Conrad's verbal portraits there is usually a predominance of one color, either in the literal sense (as with Jim's whiteness or Wait's blackness) or in a key word or phrase which defines the character through an instantaneous impression (e.g., Jim's *boyish* aspect, his bulllike pose of aggressiveness, Nostromo's shining silver buttons, or Singleton's white beard "tucked under the top button of his glistening coat").

But how does Conrad translate the visual impressions of his protagonists into portraits of *living* men and women? . . . Conrad's is a dynamic painting that keeps growing and changing almost supernaturally, like the sorcerous portrait of Dorian Gray. With each scene, each narrative point of view, a significant detail is added to the layer of color upon the surface. These little additions, at first hardly noticeable, to the initial visual impression of the protagonist finally determine both his outward appearance and his inner essence. Marlow, Conrad's most conscientious portraitist, wrestles with the artist's dilemma: "All this happened in much less time than it takes to tell, since I am trying to interpret for you into slow speech the *instantaneous effect of visual impressions.*" The latter are the main reason for Marlow's fondness of Jim: "I *watched* the youngster there. I *liked* his *appearance;* I knew his *appearance;* he came from the right place; he was one of us."

Mere appearance, however, is not enough—this is the main thrust of the novel; this is the gist of its ambivalence. What we *see* with our eyes does not necessarily correspond to the inner truth of the man. . . .

CONRAD BEGINS A PORTRAIT OF JIM IN BROAD STROKES

Marlow's visual impression of Jim is misleading, although it is not followed by sarcastic comments: "I tell you I ought to know the right kind of looks. I would have trusted the deck to that youngster on the strength of a single *glance,* and gone to sleep with both *eyes*—and, by Jove!–it wouldn't have been safe. There are depths of horror in that thought. He *looked* as genuine as a new sovereign, but there was some infernal *alloy in his metal.*"

What did Jim actually *look* like? Let us examine the method of the description in its painterly aspect. Conrad first introduces Jim from the omniscient point of vantage of the author: "He was an inch, perhaps two, under six feet, powerfully built, and he advanced straight at you with a slight stoop of the shoulders, head forward, and a fixed-from under stare which made you think of a charging bull." This is no more than a charcoal sketch as it were of Jim and the overall impression he made on the observer. A dash of color is added, to fortify this first positive impression: "He was spotlessly neat, apparelled in *immaculate white* from shoes to hat." Conrad then tells us of Jim's present occupation and his "exquisite sensibility" which made him leave his job so often. We are given a brief history of his early life and his father's parsonage. Here we pause for a snapshot (a long shot) of the latter, suggesting a watercolor sketch suitable for a postcard. . . .

Now that we have this postcard sketch, we naturally place the neatly attired, aggressively postured Jim against the idyllic background of the parsonage. The authorial voice proceeds to inform us of Jim's training and his dreams. As in the opening pictorial introduction, no precise details are provided, perhaps because Conrad wants the view of Jim to be as misty as the young man's vision of himself. The portrait is beginning to grow. We have been given a long shot of Jim, showing the outline of his body and Jim's early home at the parsonage but no exact or clear description of his parents. . . .

CONRAD GRADUALLY ADDS DETAILS TO THE PORTRAIT

If the picture of Jim is not clear so far, it is because Conrad the painter merely creates a series of first impressions of his man—from a distance. Later on, he will give us some details; he will zoom in, in a sense, for a dramatic effect. Later on, when the portrait is half complete, he will mention a book by title and even mention the color and the shape of its binding along with its price and Jim's own critical evaluation of the book. As Jim sets out for Patusan, he carries with him some books, thus described by Marlow: "I saw three books in the tumble; two small, in dark covers, and a thick green-and-gold volume—a half-crown complete Shakespeare. 'You read this?' I asked. 'Yes. Best thing to cheer up a fellow,' he said, hastily. I was struck by this appreciation, but there was no time for Shakespearean talk."

Jim takes his revolver along but forgets to take the two boxes of cartridges. He does not forget his volume of Shakespeare. Suddenly, the mist about Jim is somewhat dispelled; now we have the image of a "Hamletian" youth carrying a thick volume of the Bard's works into the unknown, into the wilderness of remote Patusan, which will prove for him to be Hamlet's "undiscovered country from whose bourne no traveler returns." Suddenly, too, Jim's dreams have acquired "a local habitation and a name" by being identified with this literary source and Jim's attitude toward it. The portrait of Jim has changed substantially.

In chapter 4 Conrad takes us to the courtroom where the official inquiry is taking place. He begins with Jim's marvelously vivid and symbolic illustration of his *Patna* experience: "She went over whatever it was as easy as a snake crawling over a stick." At this point the narrative is still conducted by Conrad's authorial voice, which chooses to throw in, rather casually, one more detail of Jim's appearance: "He stood *elevated* in the witness-box, with *burning* cheeks in a *cool* lofty room." Two ironic contrasts are intended here. Jim is about to be degraded, humiliated, and *lowered* in his own eyes, yet in terms of visual relationships in the courtroom tableau he occupies both a central and a *higher* position than anyone else, even higher than that of his penitent judge—Brierly himself. The color of his cheeks is the symbolic color of shame. Conrad the painter freezes this picture for our eyes: "the big framework of punkahs[1] moved gently to and fro above his head, and from *below* many eyes were looking at him out of *dark* faces, out of *white* faces, out of faces attentive, spellbound, as if all these people sitting in *orderly* rows upon *narrow* benches had been *enslaved* by the fascination of his voice.". . .

As the inquiry drags on and Jim's utterance becomes painful and irrelevant, the author-painter returns to his task of making us see not only Jim's moral predicament but view him with our own eyes: "*fair* of face, *big* of frame, with *young gloomy* eyes, he held his shoulders *upright* above the box while his soul writhed within him." Now Conrad's roaming eye goes back to the courtroom tableau, revealing a

---

1. fans made from palm fronds or fabric, moved by servants

few more details about the appearance of both the natives and the Europeans, and then suddenly we find ourselves looking at the crowded room through "Jim's eyes, wandering in the intervals of his answers." They rest upon the aloof Marlow, and Marlow's eyes meet his. Thus, while we the spectator-readers are not allowed to see Jim too clearly yet, Marlow, who is now being introduced by Conrad, "showed himself willing to remember Jim, to remember him at length, *in detail* and audibly." The familiar tableau of Marlow as storyteller follows immediately. Now Marlow will take over the narrator's role, after a good spread and with a box of cigars handy. . . .

Like the introductory authorial description, [Marlow's view of Jim] is a kind of a long or medium shot of the "*immobile, upstanding, broad-shouldered* youth [who] . . . just stared into the sunshine. . . . There he stood *clean-limbed, clean-faced, firm* on his feet as *promising* a boy as the sun ever shone on. . . . He had no business to *look so sound.*" It is some thirty pages later, in the embarrassing confrontation with Marlow that Marlow reveals, again somewhat casually, another important aspect of Jim's appearance, which contributes to a better understanding of his character: "The red of his *fair sunburnt complexion* deepened suddenly under the *down* of his cheeks, invaded his forehead, spread to the roots of his *curly* hair. His ears became intensely crimson, and even the *clear blue* of his eyes was darkened." The visual portrait keeps growing. Not only are his eyes clear blue; they are also "unabashed and impenetrable eyes." At this point Marlow explains how he went about his business of "painting the portrait of Jim": "I don't pretend I understood him. The *views* he let me have of himself were like those *glimpses* through the shifting rents in a thick fog—*bits of vivid and vanishing detail,* giving no *connected idea* of the general aspect of a country. They fed one's curiosity without satisfying it; they were no good for purposes of orientation. Upon the whole he was *misleading.*"

This is precisely the aim of Conrad's portraiture: Jim's immaculate white apparel, the freshness and soundness of his youthful demeanor, the bullish trustworthiness of his appearance are *meant* to be equivocal. And this piecemeal, near-idolatrous iconography of Jim, interspersed with the tragicomical accounts of the *Patna* affair and the inquiry, provide a sharply ironic contrast of white and black, enhancing the ambiguity of Jim's conception. Marlow goes on painting Jim with numerous references to his ability or inability to *see* him clearly: "I can easily *picture* him to myself in the *peopled gloom* of the cavernous place with the *light* of the bulk-lamp falling on a small portion of the bulkhead. . . . I can *see* him *glaring* at the iron, startled by the falling rust, *over-burdened* by the knowledge of an imminent death."

CONRAD FUSES OUTER AND INNER DESCRIPTIONS OF JIM

The outer and inner descriptions are fused as Marlow's portrait keeps developing: "I had another *glimpse* through *a rent in the mist* in which he moved and *had his being.* The dim candle spluttered within the ball of glass, and that was all I had to *see* him by; at his back was the *dark night* with the clear stars, whose distant *glitter* disposed in retreating planes lured the *eye* into the depths of *a greater darkness;* and yet a *mysterious light* seemed to *show* me his *boyish* head, as if in that *moment* the youth within him had, for a moment, *gleamed* and *expired.*"

As we can observe, Jim's outward aspect and his inner essence are again captured in terms Marlow's more distinct glimpses allowed by the special lighting effects cast upon Jim's *"boyish"* head—another important detail thrown in at this time. . . .

Again and again Marlow provides us with symbolic views of Jim standing either in the light of a candle or the sun or on the brink of "vast obscurity," summarizing his visual portrait, fittingly, on a note of ambiguity: "That was my *last view* of him—in *strong light,* dominating, and yet in complete accord with his surroundings . . . I own that I was *impressed,* but I must admit to myself that after all this is not the *lasting impression.* . . . I *looked* at him, *distinct and black,* planted solidly upon the shores of *a sea of light.* At the moment of *great brilliance* the *darkness* leaped back with a culminating crash, and he *vanished* before my *dazzled eyes* as utterly as though he had been blown to atoms."

As if he wanted to complete his portrait with a repetition of a symbolic touch of color, Jim's white-apparelled form opens and ends the narrative. Marlow takes us back to the first view of him, superimposing a few colors and shapes to enhance his subject's mystery: "I had never seen Jim look so *grave,* so *self-possessed,* in an *impenetrable, impressive* way. In the midst of these dark-faced men, his *stalwart* figure in *white apparel*, the *gleaming* clusters of his *fair* hair, seemed to catch all the *sunshine* that trickled through the cracks of the *closed shutters* of that dim hall, with its walls of mat, and a roof of thatch. He *appeared* like a creature not only of *another kind* but of *another essence*."

But, of course, the painting is not quite done; the kaleidoscope of visual impressions keeps on turning, each one progressively more dismal, growing more remote, growing more enigmatic, always presented in a contrasting image of light and dark, to baffle the spectator-reader, to dazzle him with the brilliance of Jim's light, to shock him with the darkness of his irrevocable fate. Marlow complains that he could never see Jim clearly, that Jim was no more than an illusion, "a strange and melancholy illusion, evolved half-consciously like all our illusions . . . visions of remote *unattainable truth, seen dimly*." The last, really last vision of Jim, as Marlow leaves him in Patusan, again reiterates the initial image: "He was *white* from head to foot, and remained *persistently visible* with the stronghold of the *night* at his back, the sea at his feet, the opportunity by his side—still *veiled*. . . . *Was it still veiled?* I don't know. For me that *white figure* in the stillness of coast and sea seemed to stand at the heart of a vast *enigma*."

Here we begin to follow Conrad's narrator as his eye turns into a moving camera, and we perceive Jim from an ever-increasing distance: "The *twilight* was ebbing fast from the sky *above* his head, the strip of sand had sunk already *under* his feet, he himself *appeared* no bigger than a child—then only a speck, a tiny *white speck*, that *seemed* to catch all the *light* left in a *darkened* world. . . . And, suddenly, I lost him."

We must now do what Marlow has done, as he explains it in a letter to "the privileged man": "I put it down here for you as though I had been an *eyewitness*. My information was *fragmentary*, but I've *fitted the pieces together*, and there is enough of them to make *an intelligible picture*."

THE FINISHED PORTRAIT

A picture of Jim is what Conrad had in mind, after all. And he has given us a veritable gallery of pictures as well as reels of film, showing fragmentary glimpses, views, and movements of his protagonist and those who came in contact with him. At the end of the novel, he asks every reader to emulate Marlow's example by fitting the fragments together to form his own intelligible picture, though, like Marlow, he may find it to be "the detailed and amazing impression of a dream." The central painting of the novel is done. The last visual glimpse of the hero is as equivocal as the first one, which is as it should be, for such was the artistic intent of the novelist-painter. The reality of his canvas must present Jim's *shadowy* ideal of conduct *and* his *eternal* constancy: the image of the inscrutable and forgotten Jim, yet also the one so well remembered by Marlow; the young man *under a cloud,* but also *one of us;* an overwhelmingly real *and* disembodied spirit. The novel ends on a note of interrogation, as it begins with an inquiry into the perplexing *Patna* case: "Who knows?" It is the final invitation to the reader to embark on yet another investigation of Jim, yet another attempt to piece together all the impressions, views, glimpses conveyed to us by Marlow. If there is still any doubt that Conrad intended those impressions to be *paintings,* perhaps these words might dispel it: "*sight* of *the Patna* . . . like a *picture* created by *fancy on canvas* . . . with its life arrested in an *unchanging light* . . . forever suspended in their expression. . . . I am certain of them. They exist as if under an enchanter's wand."

Yes, they do. As if by magic, the "mere images" have been symbolically marshalled to do battle, to challenge first our sight then our faculties of analysis, turning our fleeting impressions into a more permanent synthesis—the final, our very own portrait of Lord Jim.

I have given some illustrations, mainly from one novel, but many more can be found throughout Conrad's fiction. . . . "Mr. Conrad," observed Edwin Muir [2] in 1924, "writes in pictures, for the pictures come, and what he shows us is not action, but a progression of dissolving scenes, continuous and living, which in the end reflect action and give us a true apprehension of it." The final paragraph of Conrad's artistic credo, with which I began my argument, once more emphasizes the terms related to the making of pictures (e.g., sight, vision, form, look):

> To arrest, for the *space* of a breath the hands busy about the work of the earth, and compel men entranced by the *sight* of distant goals to *glance* for a moment at the surrounding *vision* of *form* and *colour,* of sunshine and shadows; to make them pause for a *look,* for a sigh, for a smile—such is the aim, difficult and evanescent and reserved only for a very few to

---

2. British novelist, poet, and critic

achieve. But sometimes, by the deserving and the fortunate, even that task is accomplished. And when it is accomplished—behold!—all the truth of life is there: a moment of *vision*, a sigh, a smile—and the return to an eternal rest.

Conrad, I believe, is among those very few writers who have accomplished that task. The artistic lie of his canvases has made us *see* the truth of life.

Gender Roles in Conrad's Novels

Cedric Watts

Cedric Watts argues that Conrad's characters are complex, acknowledging that to a modern audience they may appear to adhere to old-fashioned gender roles. Watts identifies recurring male and female character types and explains how Conrad uses these stereotypical characters to enhance his themes and expose injustices in the patriarchal system. Cedric Watts is the author of the critical works *The Deceptive Text: An Introduction to Covert Plots, Conrad's 'Heart of Darkness': A Critical and Contextual Discussion, Joseph Conrad: 'Nostromo,'* and a biography, *Joseph Conrad: A Literary Life.*

Editor's Note: The author of this article uses the following abbreviations to identify Conrad's works: *AF—Almayer's Folly;* HD—"Heart of Darkness"; *NN—The Nigger of the 'Narcissus'; N—Nostromo; R—The Rescue; UWE—Under Western Eyes; V—Victory.*

Conrad's works cumulatively imply a model of admirable masculine conduct: it is chivalric and gentlemanly in its combination of courage, dignity, reticence and respect for traditions of service; it is stoical, too, in the readiness to engage in struggle without confidence in victory; and sceptical in its view of human nature and history. Such an ethical ideal is implicit in the depiction of Marlow and of various anonymous narrators, or is epitomised by such memorable minor characters as the French lieutenant in *Lord Jim*; and it is implicit in the self-image of Conrad as depicted in his various autobiographical writings.

UNUSUAL PLOT AND CHARACTERIZATION

Conrad often likes to work against the grain, however; invoking a convention only to question or complicate or subvert it. If he shows an Achilles, his interest lies in the Achilles' heel. Lord Jim, for instance, looks like a romantic hero—yet he has been partly corrupted by his very dreams of being a romantic hero. The vulnerability of virtue (or its short-sightedness) is one of Conrad's preoccupations; so is his sense of tentacular vice, which sends out a tentacle to grip the seemingly sound and good. Thus, some of his heroes are drawn into complicity with corrupt kindred: Jim with Gentleman Brown, Marlow with Kurtz, Heyst with Jones. Characters may be paired (albeit briefly) in ways which question the initial sense of contrast between them: Gould and Hernández, Decoud and Hirsch. Just as Conrad subverts orthodox principles of plot-structure by 'building holes' (ellipses, elisions, perspectival shifts and chronological jumps) into his plots, so he is sometimes capable of building holes into characterisation by leaving opaque or mysterious those areas which orthodox writers would fill with ample biographical information.

In his major works, the manipulations and fracturings of plot give enhanced importance to thematic connections, and the interlinkages established between characters give enhanced importance to the sense of moral and psychological patterning within events, or to a sense of the ironic workings of history. To compare is to contrast; to contrast is to compare. By the networks of connections between characters, Conrad draws attention not only to individual distinctiveness (and often to human isolation and incomprehension) but also to ironic likeness and common needs.

Conrad can be an acute psychologist, not so much by any profound depiction of an individual's psychology as by his concentration on forces operating variously within particular groupings. *The Nigger of the 'Narcissus'*, for example, dramatises the difficulty of distinguishing a vicarious self-pity (which divides people) from an altruistic co-operation (which unites them): even the wise captain briefly but dangerously confuses the two, as he later recognises. In 'Heart of Darkness', we are invited to realise the full extent of the moral hollowness in 'civilised' men: even the apparently heroic Kurtz proves 'hollow at the core'. In *Nostromo*, we are shown how men habitually idealise the material world in which they are ambushed and are tantalised by their own ideals.

CONRAD'S WOMEN

In his treatment of women, as we shall see, Conrad offers a
diversity of recurrent types. They variously express male
observations, beliefs, hopes, fears and fantasies, and sometimes provide a basis for criticism of masculine limitations.
The female counterpart to his recurrent 'gentlemanly' type
is, significantly, one in which selfless service (often to a
man or men, within a male-dominated world) is a prominent feature. Nevertheless, when Conrad is describing sub-
servient daughters or apparently loyal wives, he frequently
notes concealed features which make those females potentially rebellious against their fathers or husbands; as so
often, he likes to imply that individuals are largely opaque to
each other and that the bonds of solidarity are weaker than
people may suppose.

Some of Conrad's women are associated with the jungle,
dark and fecund, while others are likened to statues, impos-
ingly beautiful. This dichotomy may be seen as a post-
Darwinian version of the traditional literary 'rose and lily'
(or 'whore and madonna') pairings which have been
assailed by feminists for their apparent denial of an integrated female personality. In addition, Conrad sometimes
imagines the symbolic or actual interchangeability of
women and wealth. (Here he partly anticipates Claude Lévi-
Strauss's notions of females as objects of social exchange.)
Thus, in the first novel, *Almayer's Folly*, as Nina turns more
and more from her father to Dain, so Dain's wealth flows
into Mrs Almayer's hidden coffer; and Almayer's loss of Nina
entails the destruction of his hopes of finding treasure in the
hinterland. In *Nostromo*, Gould's love for the silver of the
mine gradually supersedes his love for his childless wife,
who comes to see him as surrounded by 'a circumvallation'
of precious metal; he even sleeps at the mine, with the silver.
In 'A Smile of Fortune', the hero finds Alice Jacobus so
seductive that, to be alone with her, he enters into a dis-
tasteful business deal with her father; he loses the young
woman but unexpectedly makes a big profit. 'I dreamt of a
pile of gold in the form of a grave in which a girl was buried,
and woke up callous with greed.' Repeatedly, sexual and
emotional relationships are tainted, corrupted or subverted
by 'material interests'.

Among Conrad's prominent male and female characters,

it is easy to discern some recurrent types. Predictably, given the historical context of his writings, females in this list are usually defined in relationship to males, whereas males are usually defined in relationship to work and career-goals.

RECURRING MALE CHARACTERS

1. THE HAMLETS.[1] Examples: Decoud (*N*), Hefst (*V*), D'Alcacer (*R*). Civilised, sceptical, reflective, and likely to become immobilised at some point of crisis.

2. THE QUIXOTES.[2] Examples: Lingard of *Almayer's Folly*, *An Outcast* and *The Rescue*, and Captain Anthony in *Chance*. However, all Conrad's active idealists partake of the quixotic: they pursue goals which recede or prove illusory, or they succeed only at the price of a kind of monomania which may result in suffering or destruction for themselves or others. This category includes the men of egoistic imagination, such as Almayer (*AF*), Kurtz (*HD*) and Gould (*N*): visionaries who may be led to disaster by their vision.

3. THE SYMPATHETIC NARRATORS. None of Conrad's fictional narrators (and possibly not even the narrators of some of his non-fictional writings) should automatically be equated with Conrad. But biographically some of the first-person narrators (particularly some who are anonymous sea-captains) stand very close to the author, having had experiences which relate closely to those of the younger Conrad. Examples are the narrators of *The Shadow-Line*, 'Falk', 'The Secret Sharer' and 'A Smile of Fortune': anonymous yet congruent and continuous (having a consistent common identity), recalling past voyages and encounters; fallible but likeable, curious about life, gentlemanly, but (in important respects) unconventionally tolerant and broad-minded.

A narrator who is carefully individuated and is more distinct from the author than the foregoing figures is, of course, Charles Marlow. The most convincing, intelligent and interesting of Conrad's characters is the Marlow of 'Heart of Darkness', followed closely by the Marlow of *Lord Jim*, at some distance by the Marlow of 'Youth' and at a much greater distance by the Marlow of *Chance*. In 'Heart of Darkness' and *Lord Jim* Marlow is perceptive, sceptical and reflective, but, unlike the Hamlets (our Type 1), he is able to respond bravely to crises—he is a survivor; he has the imag-

---

1. based on Shakespeare's Hamlet   2. based on Cervantes' Don Quixote

ination of Type 2, but also moral stability and (by the standards of his times) a humane liberalism of outlook. He shares the romantic adventurousness of the quixotic type while retaining a critical spirit. As a former *Conway* cadet and ex-captain, he is also a reasonably prosperous English gentleman of the upper middle class who likes the sound of his own voice and can be patronising. The Marlow of 'Youth' is rather sentimental—perhaps slightly the worse for drink; and the Marlow of *Chance* is old, garrulous and at times abrasively male-chauvinistic.

4. THE STALWART WORKERS. Examples: Singleton (*NN*), the boilermaker (*HD*), Captain MacWhirr and Solomon Rout ('Typhoon'), Don Pepe (*N*), Jörgensen (*R*), and perhaps Davidson (*V*). Not articulate, bright or imaginative, but industrious and utterly reliable: they know their job and stick to it conscientiously even when others fail. They embody the Victorian work-ethic, the seaman's code, and hard primitivism.

5. THE PROFESSIONAL ÉLITE. Examples: the French lieutenant in *Lord Jim* (and possibly Brierly and Stein in the same novel), Captain Allistoun in *The Nigger*, the engineer-in-chief in *Nostromo*, and Captain Giles in *The Shadow-Line*. These are the aristocracy of their professions: men of maturity, courage, integrity and wisdom, though they too may be laconic or gnomic in utterance. . . .

6. THE EXOTIC PRINCE, CHIEFTAIN OR WARRIOR. Examples: Dain Maroola in *Almayer's Folly*, Arsat in 'The Lagoon', Karain in 'Karain', Dain Waris in *Lord Jim* and Hassim in *The Rescue*. Such men are brown, handsome, noble, brave and apparently virile, though susceptible to being unmanned by a woman. They may be helped or brought to disaster by the white friends who patronise them. While their fictional location is the Malay Archipelago of the period 1870–90, they anticipate a stock type in the Hollywood jungle-movies of the period 1920–50.

RECURRING FEMALE CHARACTERS

1. EXOTIC SEDUCTRESSES. Examples: Nina (*AF*), Aissa (*An Outcast*), Kurtz's consort (*HD*). They are associated with the fecund jungle of which they may seem an emanation; potent and with the effect of weakening or incapacitating the men who embrace them, as though primitive nature were taking its revenge on the civilised or as though the dark and femi-

nine were taking its revenge on the white and masculine .

2. NOBLE IDEALISTS. Examples: Kurtz's Intended (*HD*), Antonia (*N*), Natalia Haldin (*UWE*). These are radiant romantic idealists who preserve their faith in the men they love but who, to a large extent, are ignorant of those men or of the harsh realities of the world.

3. THE STATUESQUELY BEAUTIFUL OBJECT OF MALE DESIRE. Examples: Hermann's niece ('Falk'), Felicia Moorsom ('The Planter of Malata'), Doña Rita (*Arrow of Gold*), Mrs Travers (*R*). They are associated, in the last three instances, with some of Conrad's most disappointingly conventional writing.

4. THE SEEMINGLY SUBJUGATED. Examples: Mrs Hervey in 'The Return', Winnie Verloc in *The Secret Agent*, Alice Jacobus ('A Smile of Fortune'), Flora Barral in *Chance*, Lena in *Victory*, Arlette of *The Rover*. These are women with unhappy pasts who are or have been so strongly dominated by men that their inner natures seem to have been crushed or suppressed, but who are yet capable of displaying surprising independence: they may strike back.

5. THE LADY ALMONERS.[3] Examples: Mrs Gould in the later stages of *Nostromo* and both Tekla and Natalia Haldin at the end of *Under Western Eyes*. These are idealistic women who have had disillusioning experience of the world but who still, in their limited sphere, do what they can to make the world a better place. (This was a stock type in Victorian literature: George Eliot's Dorothea and Romola are famous instances.)

FEMINIST CRITICISMS OF CONRAD

In the decades following the publication of Kate Millett's *Sexual Politics* (1970), feminism burgeoned, transforming cultural history by revealing the appalling extent to which masculist assumptions had hitherto been accepted as generally valid. Eventually feminist literary critics turned their scrutiny upon Conrad. A standard feminist approach is to search literary texts of past eras for evidence of male chauvinism, particularly the stereotyping of female characters in demeaning ways. Predictably, Conrad was usually found guilty; 'predictably', because only a minority of fiction-writers before 1970 (whether male or female) could fulfil the exacting and sometimes anachronistic requirements of latter-day feminists.

3. those who distribute alms

There were some extenuating claims. Ruth Nadelhaft, for example, argued that in Conrad's fiction women are centres of intelligent resistance to male vanity and imperialist assumptions: 'Conrad wrote through the critical eyes of women characters.' Other critics were, however, antagonized by 'Heart of Darkness'. Nina Pelikan Straus declared that this novella is 'brutally sexist': male critics have repeatedly become accomplices of Marlow, who 'brings truth to men by virtue of his bringing falsehood to women':

> The woman reader . . . is in the position to suggest that Marlow's cowardice consists of his inability to face the dangerous self that is the form of his own masculinist vulnerability: his own complicity in the racist, sexist, imperialist, and finally libidinally satisfying world he has inhabited with Kurtz.

Elaine Showalter said that the tale assumed a distinctively male 'circle of readers'; explicitly and implicitly, it excludes females from knowledge of reality. Johanna M. Smith declared that 'Heart of Darkness' 'reveals the collusion of imperialism and patriarchy: Marlow's narrative aims to "colonize" and "pacify" both savage darkness and women'. This echoed the main point of Bette London's discussion of the same tale. London argued that Marlow is clearly a male chauvinist. . . . Furthermore, Marlow's narrative 'puts Marlow in the feminine place, literally, the space of Kurtz's Intended', and even 'puts his audience in Marlow's former place: the place of the feminine'.

CONRAD'S DEPICTION OF MEN AND WOMEN

Within these radical readings, some of the claims seem excessive for want of due historical consideration. By the standards of its own times, 'Heart of Darkness' was a courageously interrogative text; and present-day critics become ideologically narcissistic if they belabour all those past literary works which do not reflect today's ideological preferences or prejudices. Some of the recurrent types discernible in Conrad's depiction of both men and women were recognisable in reality in his time; some remain so in ours. Males as well as females are frequent objects of his ironic and satirical observation; and, not seldom in Conrad's fiction, women are shown to be more perceptive and less self-centred than the men who dominate their world: examples include Nina in *Almayer's Folly*, Emilia in *Nostromo*, Tekla in *Under Western Eyes* and

Lena in *Victory*. If women usually occupy subordinate roles in his works, this is partly a reflection of the historical facts of his day. Feminist critics who oppose the principle of stereotyping when it concerns female characters sometimes espouse that very principle when, seeking to stereotype an author as a 'male chauvinist', they envisage in the texts the demeaning features they wish to castigate.

Undoubtedly, Conrad's works often reveal some familiar masculine fears and limitations when women are depicted. As we have seen, the sexually potent woman is often seen as subversive, her male partner as a person unmanned or entrapped by sexual experience. (This was a common literary theme in Conrad's day: the relationship between Gudrun and Gerald in Lawrence's *Women in Love* provides a vivid illustration.) Marital relations more often resemble a trap than a liberation into fulfilment. The sea-captain who takes his wife aboard is rendered unreliable by divided allegiances (as is shown in 'Youth' and 'The Secret Sharer'). Captain Beard in 'Youth' declares: 'A sailor has no business with a wife'; and Captain Mitchell in *Nostromo* concurs: 'I was never married myself. A sailor should exercise self-denial.' . . .

Marlow does at least (contradicting his opinion in 'Heart of Darkness') claim that whereas men live in a 'fool's paradise', women see 'the whole truth'. Another mitigating factor in *Chance* is the portrayal of Carleon Anthony, who is partly based on Coventry Patmore, author of *The Angel in the House*. Carleon is a writer who sentimentalises woman (as domestic angel) in his poetry, but is a tyrant in the home; a partial counterpart to the hypocritical Peter Ivanovitch who, in *Under Western Eyes*, poses as a feminist in his writings but treats his female secretary with ruthless contempt. From 'The Idiots' to *The Secret Agent*, from Willems in *An Outcast* to Schomberg in *Victory*, Conrad critically portrayed the domestic (often sexual) servitude which a husband imposes on his wife. Almost a century before marital rape was made a crime in Britain, Conrad had portrayed the woman's ordeal frankly and sympathetically in 'The Idiots'. Even the cumbrously experimental tale, 'The Return', tries to depict the collapse of a chauvinistic husband's delusions as his desperate wife declares: 'I've a right—a right to—to—myself . . .' In *Victory*, Lena (before dying self-sacrificially) suffers in turn the bullying sexual demands of Schomberg, the diffident sexuality of Heyst, an attempted rape by Ricardo and some pathological misogyny from Jones; so the text amply reveals the collusions and contradictions of male dominance. Conrad frequently directed his scepticism against patriarchal authority of various kinds, whether divine or human.

In short, although feminists have substantial grounds for seeking to stereotype Conrad as 'patriarchal', Conrad's works often remind us that a stereotype is a manipulable simplification of a more complex original. Meanwhile, the feminist endeavour to expose the strategies of power may have consequences that Conrad would have applauded. It is now widely recognised that, for centuries, society has inscribed women with submissive characterization; and, as a result, millions of women have led stunted lives. Similarly, for centuries, society has inscribed men with aggressive characterisation; and, as a result, millions of men have died on battlefields. The study of fiction is increasingly being recognised as the study of social authority. Texts like *Nostromo* offer paradigms—conspicuous models—of social inscription, and they offer warnings about such inscription. Literary studies may obliquely help to liberate individuals from the grip of socially-imposed and inflexible characterisation.

CHAPTER 2

Conrad's Short Works

READINGS ON
JOSEPH CONRAD

Imagination and Character in *Typhoon*

Jeremy Hawthorn

Jeremy Hawthorn argues that in *Typhoon* Conrad
explores the theme of imagination. At the beginning,
MacWhirr lacks imagination and acts only on what
he knows—facts. During a typhoon, Hawthorn maintains, MacWhirr acquires the capacity to sympathize
with and inspire his crew and the ability to visualize
the possible destruction of his ship. Jeremy Hawthorn
is professor of modern British literature at the
University of Trondheim in Norway. He is the author
of *Joseph Conrad: Language and Fictional Self-
Consciousness* and *A Glossary of Contemporary
Literary Theory*.

In *Typhoon, Under Western Eyes*, and 'The Tale' central characters are faced with the problem of making sense of the
world from limited information, of constructing a picture of
some sort of totality from isolated clues. Thus in different
ways all of these works explore the functioning and the limits of human imagination. . . .

In *Typhoon* the problem of interpretation occurs at different levels: MacWhirr has to make sense of the omens of bad
weather that are presented to him. . . .

Typhoon 'is a study of a hero who thinks and operates on
a purely factual level'.[1] Land's case is a strong one, and
Typhoon in its early pages certainly gives the impression of
being a work written to explore a particular formula.

> Having just enough imagination to carry him through each
> successive day, and no more, he was tranquilly sure of him-
> self; and from the very same cause he was not in the least
> conceited. It is your imaginative superior who is touchy, over-
> bearing, and difficult to please; but every ship Captain
> MacWhirr commanded was the floating abode of harmony

---

1. from Stephen K. Land's *Conrad and the Paradox of Plot*

and peace. It was, in truth, as impossible for him to take a flight of fancy as it would be for a watchmaker to put together a chronometer with nothing except a two-pound hammer and a whip-saw in the way of tools. Yet the uninteresting lives of men so entirely given to the actuality of the bare existence have their mysterious side.

If the opening sentences of this passage seem to suggest that Conrad is more interested in exploring a thesis than creating a complex character, the final quoted sentence indicates that perhaps something more than this can be expected. We should note that it is MacWhirr's *life* rather than his consciousness which we are told may be more complex and obscure than might be expected: one of the lessons suggested by *Typhoon* is that the process of active living, of grappling with problems along with one's fellows, may be creative of mental profundity in even the most unimaginative. . . . *Typhoon* gives us one whose lack of imagination does not render him immune to the educative powers of experience, especially when this experience is of an extreme kind.

Land also suggests that Mr Jukes, the chief mate, 'is a paler version of Jim, a young, relatively inexperienced, but highly promising officer endowed with a hyperactive imagination.' We are reminded that Jim was also a chief mate.

The opening pages of *Typhoon*, then, present us with a pair of rather schematically drawn characters, characters seemingly created to explore a thesis rather than to present human life in its full complexity and contradictoriness. And yet from this rather simplistic opening the work moves to a far more complex and rich exploration of a range of recognizable Conradian issues: the functioning of the imagination; the educative power of experience; human solidarity and human isolation; work as an escape from isolation and as a route to the discovery of the truth about oneself, others and the world; and an attempt to isolate those factors which enable (or prevent) effective human communication.

Part of the artificiality involved in the creation of a character totally lacking in imagination is avoided, or disguised, by portraying Captain MacWhirr as an eccentric who is perceived as such by his fellow officers. . . .

Failures of insight on Jukes's part lead the reader to treat his ensuing account of MacWhirr with some circumspection. And after this account is finished, an authorial narrative comment reinforces the reader's sense that Jukes's view of MacWhirr is not necessarily to be relied upon. . . .

> The sea itself, as if sharing Mr Jukes's good-natured forbear-
> ance, had never put itself out to startle the silent man, who
> seldom looked up, and wandered innocently over the waters
> with the only visible purpose of getting food, raiment, and
> house-room for three people ashore.

What we are led to expect from this passage is that when it
does put itself out, the sea may well discover depths in
MacWhirr invisible to Jukes, perhaps, indeed, still only
potentialities waiting to be called into existence by the
typhoon. MacWhirr's lack of imagination is thus related to a
lack of extreme experiences on his part.

> He had never been given a glimpse of immeasurable strength
> and of immoderate wrath, the wrath that passes exhausted
> but never appeased—the wrath and fury of the passionate
> sea. He knew it existed, as we know that crime and abomina-
> tions exist; he had heard of it as a peaceable citizen in a town
> hears of battles, famines, and floods, and yet knows nothing
> of what these things mean—though, indeed, he may have
> been mixed up in a street row, have gone without his dinner
> once, or been soaked to his skin in a shower. Captain
> MacWhirr had sailed over the surface of the oceans as some
> men go skimming over the years of existence to sink gently
> into a placid grave, ignorant of life to the last, without ever
> having been made to see all it may contain of perfidy, of vio-
> lence, and of terror. There are on sea and land such men thus
> fortunate—or thus disdained by destiny or the sea.

MacWhirr's lack of imagination, then, is not innate: it is at
least in part the product of his not ever having been made
aware of the extremes of experience life can hold. . . .

MACWHIRR'S LIMITATIONS IN LANGUAGE

Because of his lack of imagination, signs do not bring a distant reality to his mind. His response to language is—at the
start of the work at any rate—similar to his response to other
signs. 'Omens were as nothing to him, and he was unable to
discover the message of a prophecy till the fulfillment had
brought it home to his very door'. MacWhirr believes that
'facts can speak for themselves with overwhelming precision', and writes home

> from the Coast of China twelve times every year, desiring
> quaintly to be 'remembered to the children,' and subscribing
> himself 'your loving husband,' as calmly as if the words so
> long used by so many men were, apart from their shape,
> worn-out things, and of a faded meaning.

But how can MacWhirr expect to be understood through his written words by his wife, when he himself cannot use words to conjure up an absent, not concretely experienced reality? The language MacWhirr understands is the language of facts, and in making this point, *Typhoon* draws attention to the differential manner in which MacWhirr treats facts and words. . . .

For MacWhirr facts, not words, are eloquent, speaking in the clear and definite language that MacWhirr does not find in books. And of course to have one's interest restricted to immediate facts inevitably entails a limited perception of possible future events. . . .

THE TYPHOON FORCES MACWHIRR TO CHANGE

So far *Typhoon* sounds very much like a *roman à thèse*, a work written to illustrate a set of ideas in which the characters are puppets subordinated to their task of exemplifying certain issues. That *Typhoon* is actually much more than this can be attributed to the fact that it is also a study of *change*, of human development attendant upon the extreme experiences recounted in the work. It is only comparatively recently that such a view of the work has gained acceptance among Conrad critics. In his book *Theories of Action in Conrad*, Francis Hubbard argues that the crucial experience for MacWhirr is that he foresees the possibility of losing his ship, and 'has thereby been forced to give up his belief that only present facts matter'. Hubbard cites in particular the following passages:

> 'Can't have . . . fighting . . . board ship . . .'
>
> 'Had to do what's fair by them . . . Had to do what's fair . . . Had to do what's fair, for all—they are only Chinamen. Give them the same chance with ourselves—hang it all. She isn't lost yet. Bad enough to be shut up below in a gale . . . Couldn't let that go on in my ship *if I knew she hadn't five minutes to live.*'

Forced by the typhoon to think forward to possible future eventualities, imagination is born in MacWhirr; he realizes that there is a world beyond immediate facts which can be apprehended only through signs, tokens, omens, or whatever.

> The hurricane, with its power to madden the seas, to sink ships, to uproot trees, to overturn strong walls and dash the very birds of the air to the ground, had found this taciturn man in its path, and, doing its utmost, had managed to wring out a few words. Before the renewed wrath of winds swooped on his ship, Captain MacWhirr was moved to declare, in a tone of vexation, as it were: 'I wouldn't like to lose her.'

Behind this passage lies a whole philosophy of language, a belief that it is from the demands the physical world makes on human beings that language springs, fulfilling the need human beings have to express possibilities glimpsed in extreme actualities.

MacWhirr's attitude towards books changes from frustrated dismissal to reluctant acceptance that they can tell us something about aspects of the real world hidden from us, separate from our personal experience. It is a sign of this change when MacWhirr says to Jukes that, 'According to the books the worst is not over yet'.

Two other things testify to the fact that a significant change has taken place in MacWhirr during the typhoon: his insistence that Jukes go below to stop the Chinamen fighting, and his ability to inject resolve into the despairing Jukes—to communicate fully and effectively with him. MacWhirr has earlier dismissed with contempt Jukes's use of the word 'passengers' to describe the Chinamen, using the dismissive term 'coolies' about them. And yet it is MacWhirr who worries about them during the typhoon, not Jukes, nor the boatswain who, after reporting on the situation below, 'gave no more thought to the coolies'. MacWhirr is now able to *imagine* what the reported situation is like, and what it may become, and this makes him more fully human.

> He was glad the trouble in the 'tween-deck had been discovered in time. If the ship had to go after all, then, at least, she wouldn't be going to the bottom with a lot of people in her fighting teeth and claw. That would have been odious. And in that feeling there was a humane intention and a vague sense of the fitness of things.

This passage precedes MacWhirr's thinking 'I shouldn't like to lose her' of the ship, and this suggests that his imagination has been brought into action as much by his human sympathy for the Chinamen as by his becoming aware of the possibility of losing his ship.

MacWhirr *forces* Jukes to go below to sort out the situation there. Jukes, it should be noted, is unwilling to do this because of his *excessive* imagination; he is convinced that the ship is lost. But once he has done this (and, by the way, given the crew some useful inspiration), he is in a position to receive MacWhirr's philosophy of life and to be given confidence by it.

'You are always meeting trouble half way, Jukes.' Captain MacWhirr remonstrated quaintly. 'Though it's a fact that the second mate is no good. D'ye hear, Mr Jukes? You would be left alone if. . . .'

. . . . .

'Don't you be put out by anything,' the Captain continued, mumbling rather fast. 'Keep her facing it. They may say what they like, but the heaviest seas run with the wind. Facing it—always facing it—that's the way to get through. You are a young sailor. Face it. That's enough for any man. Keep a cool head.'

'Yes sir,' said Jukes, with a flutter of the heart.

The passage has all the signs of having a meaning that is of much wider application than merely to certain questions of seamanship. Imagination is necessary; one needs to be able to interpret signs, to consider possible eventualities. But these should never leave one to forsake the sanity—and humanity—guaranteeing action of facing the immediate demands made upon one by physical and human reality. From this point on we note that all contact with MacWhirr during the typhoon serves to strengthen Jukes and to raise his spirits. Hearing the captain speak to the engine-room,

> For some reason Jukes experienced an access of confidence, a sensation that came from outside like a warm breath, and made him feel equal to every demand. The distant muttering of the darkness stole into his ears. He noted it unmoved, out of that sudden belief in himself, as a man safe in a shirt of mail would watch a point.

In case we should be in any doubt as to the source of Jukes's access of confidence, in the subsequent paragraph we find Jukes's thoughts adopting a phrase from MacWhirr: 'She rumbled in her depths, shaking a white plummet of steam into the night, and Jukes' thought skimmed like a bird through the engine-room, where Mr Rout—good man—was ready'. The 'good man' is MacWhirr's formulation, and it is indeed to Jukes's adoption of the despised MacWhirr's outlook, his obedience to his commands, that his access of confidence must be attributed. . . .

We note, however, that whilst the lessons learned by MacWhirr during the typhoon seem to have stuck, Jukes appears to revert to his old self in his final letter to the Western Ocean trade chum. Some individuals, *Typhoon* seems to suggest, can successfully internalize the requirements of a tradition, while others need the permanent support and discipline provided by a strong and living external tradition, by their fellows. . . .

THE EFFECT OF THE NARRATOR'S VOICE

Because *Typhoon* is not a pure epistolary novel but has a narrator possessed of more than human knowledge, a consistency of narrative *tone* . . . is a striking feature of *Typhoon*. The narrative voice we encounter is both pitying and sympathetic, fatalistic (even wearily so at times) and ironic.

I use the term 'possessed of more than human knowledge' rather than 'omniscient' because at times in *Typhoon* the narrator admits to ignorance.

> Yet the uninteresting lives of men so entirely given to the actuality of the bare existence have their mysterious side. It was impossible in Captain MacWhirr's case, for instance, to understand what under heaven could have induced that perfectly satisfactory son of a petty grocer in Belfast to run away to sea. And yet he had done that very thing at the age of fifteen. It was enough, when you thought it over, to give you the idea of an immense, potent, and invisible hand thrust into the ant-heaps of the earth, laying hold of shoulders, knocking heads together, and setting the unconscious faces of the multitude towards inconceivable goals and in undreamt-of directions.

The tone generated by passages such as this is crucial to the overall effect of *Typhoon* upon the reader. 'It was enough, when you thought it over': the voice of the narrator is recognizably human—expressing quizzical bemusement at MacWhirr's unexpected action but appealing to a shared pool of human experience to which both narrator and reader have access. But it is also god-like in its distanced view of the human participants in the narrative—an impression strengthened by the ant-heap example, with its talk of 'inconceivable goals' and 'undreamt-of directions'. Human beings, in this view, are necessarily ignorant of what the future holds in store for them. . . .

The repeated use of bathetic[2] similes forces *us* to use our imaginations much as the typhoon forces MacWhirr to use (or discover) his; we can no longer confine our outlook to that of the characters themselves, but have to set characters in the context of an indifferent and violent universe. Thus the very tone of *Typhoon* contributes to our sense of human limitations, of the absolute necessity for us to escape from our imprisonment by the demands of immediate experiences and to collaborate with our fellows to overcome the restrictions of our own puny intellects and foresight.

2. commonplace; anticlimactic

Symbolism in "The Secret Sharer"

J.B. Priestley

J.B. Priestley analyzes the symbolism of the captain's hat in Conrad's "The Secret Sharer." Priestley suggests that the hat has three interpretations: as a marker, as an act of kindness, and as the shadow of the captain's self. In general, the hat reinforces Conrad's theme that confronting the whole self—the dark as well as the light—is important for self-knowledge and confidence. J.B. Priestley is the author of *The Good Companions*, a novel; *Delight*, a collection of essays; and *Dangerous Corner*, a play. He is also the author of the literary history *Literature and Western Man*.

The Secret Sharer, along with two other stories, came out in a volume called *'Twixt Land and Sea*, first published in 1912. But Conrad tells us that it was written some years earlier than that date, and that the actual occurrence on which the story was based "came to light and even got into the newspapers about the middle 'eighties, though I had heard of it before, as it were privately, among the officers of the great wool fleet in which my first years in deep water were served." In short, what he calls "the basic fact" of this story had been lodged in his mind for a long time. This is important. It helps to explain the particular character of the story that he finally gave us. It was not a story that he wrote just because it seemed to him to make a good yarn. Too many people already knew something like it. A ship's captain had once secretly harbored a fellow officer who had broken arrest from another ship: the tale had been going round for years and years. That Conrad should decide to tell it meant that for him it was more than a mere yarn, more than an unusual incident in seafaring life. In his mind it had begun to take on a certain density of meaning, a significance that was certainly there but difficult to explain. Sometimes we

From J.B. Priestley, afterword to "The Secret Sharer," by Joseph Conrad (London: J.M. Dent, n.d.), as it appears in *Four English Novels*, edited by J.B. Priestley and O.B. Davis (New York: Harcourt Brace, 1960). Reprinted by permission of J.M. Dent.

79

have dreams that are like this; we cannot forget them; we feel they are important, yet cannot altogether understand them. That is because dreams are symbolical. And *The Secret Sharer*, like much of modern fiction, is symbolical too.

Just What Is Symbolism?

Therefore, in order fully to appreciate this story, we have to try to understand what symbolism is. This may be tough going, but it is well worth the effort just because so much modern literature is symbolical. *The Secret Sharer* is in fact a very good introduction to symbolism in literature. If we see how it works here, we can begin to understand how it works elsewhere. First of all, symbolism does not mean that one thing simply stands for another thing, as a figure in a picture might represent Hope or Despair. This one-thing-meaning-another-thing is allegory, not true symbolism. And while the work of many great writers and painters has been symbolical, nearly all of them have taken care to avoid allegory, which is shallow and rather boring. A true symbol can always be interpreted in several different ways. It has various meanings shading off into one another. And it always has a final deepest meaning that intellectually we cannot really grasp at all, though we feel it emotionally. (All this makes symbolic literature continually exciting, even after we have read it several times. It is like a magic bottle we can never empty.) The reason why we cannot completely grasp the deepest meaning is because it does not really belong to the conscious part of our minds but to the part below the level of consciousness, to what is called the unconscious, the part that creates our dreams for us, and does its own kind of thinking, not in ideas and words representing ideas, but in a sort of picture language.

Anything truly symbolical, then, excites both the upper conscious level of our minds and the picture-thinking unconscious level, and so at the same time forms a link between these two parts of the mind. This is why, if we are sensitive at all, a symbolical tale seems so rich in meaning and yet at the same time seems so mysterious and disturbing. We are responding to it on more than one level of the mind. We feel it is not unlike our more vivid and memorable dreams, those very dreams that we feel are so important to us and yet sound so boring when we try to tell other people about them. And we might almost say that a symbolic writer is somebody clever enough to tell us his or her dream *without* boring us. The strange magic comes through to us.

MULTIPLE MEANINGS OF THE HAT

Now let us take a good example of symbolism from *The Secret Sharer.* We could imitate Erle Stanley Gardner[1] and call it "The Case of the Captain's Hat." Let us remember what happens. Just as Leggatt is leaving him, in the dark sail locker, the captain snatches off his "floppy hat," tries to ram it on Leggatt's head. For a moment Leggatt does not understand, but then accepts the hat, shakes hands, and vanishes. In order that Leggatt can easily swim ashore, the captain has taken the ship dangerously close to the land, so close that the mate thinks all is lost. To bring the ship safely round, the captain desperately needs some mark to steer by. And when he finds it, what is it but the hat, which had fallen off Leggatt's head during his swim to the shore? So the hat helps the captain to bring his ship out of danger, and because he does this, he wins the confidence of his officers and men and increases his own self-respect. For, remember, from the first we have been told that this young captain, appointed to command a strange ship, is an unknown quantity to his officers and crew, and is by no means completely certain of himself. It is this episode of Leggatt, together with this curious incident of the hat he gave Leggatt, that finally gives the captain all that he wishes to have.

Now this hat being a symbol, we can consider it on more than one level of interpretation. If we want to be very superficial about it, we can say that giving the hat to Leggatt is a good convincing little incident in a tale of adventure, and that the hat reappearing as a useful steering mark in the water is one of those coincidences often found in tales of adventure. But few of us are likely to be satisfied with the hat on that level. So let us try again. When the captain, in that desperate moment, had a thoughtful and generous impulse to provide Leggatt with some head covering, he was finally rewarded by finding, in a later and even more desperate moment, that the hat provided him with the steering mark he needed. This gives us the simple cause-and-effect we often find in moral tales. And those readers who can remain happily on this rather cosy level should not be bullied

---

1. crime novelist and Perry Mason creator

THE CAPTAIN'S HAT

In this excerpt from Conrad's "The Secret Sharer," the captain gains the confidence of his crew when he maneuvers the ship out of a tight place by watching his hat floating on the water.

And now I forgot the secret stranger ready to depart, and remembered only that I was a total stranger to the ship. I did not know her. Would she do it? How was she to be handled?

I swung the mainyard and waited helplessly. She was perhaps stopped, and her very fate hung in the balance, with the black mass of Koh-ring[1] like the gate of the everlasting night towering over her taffrail. What would she do now? Had she way on her yet? I stepped to the side swiftly, and on the shadowy water I could see nothing except a faint phosphorescent flash revealing the glassy smoothness of the sleeping surface. It was impossible to tell—and I had not learned yet the feel of my ship. Was she moving? What I needed was something easily seen, a piece of paper, which I could throw overboard and watch. I had nothing on me. To run down for it I didn't dare. There was no time. All at once my strained, yearning stare distinguished a white object floating within a yard of the ship's side. White on the black water. A phosphorescent flash passed under it. What was that thing? . . . I recognized my own floppy hat. It must have fallen off his head . . . and he didn't bother. Now I had what I wanted—the saving mark for my eyes. . . .

And I watched the hat—the expression of my sudden pity for his mere flesh. It had been meant to save his homeless head from the dangers of the sun. And now—behold—it was saving the ship, by serving me for a mark to help out the ignorance of my strangeness. Ha! It was drifting forward, warning me just in time that the ship had gathered sternway.

'Shift the helm,' I said in a low voice to the seaman standing still like a statue. . . .

On the overshadowed deck all hands stood by the forebraces waiting for my order. The stars ahead seemed to be gliding from right to left. And all was so still in the world that I heard the quiet remark, 'She's round,' passed in a tone of intense relief between two seamen.

'Let go and haul.'

The foreyards ran round with a great noise, amidst cheery cries.

1. a small mountainous island

into leaving it. But many of us cannot help feeling that there is more in the tale, more under its hat, than this good-deed-rewarded. So let us descend, hat in hand, to a deeper, darker, more mysterious level.

Now a hat is a covering. ("And keep this under your hat," men say to each other when they are exchanging confidences.) It is an individual and very personal sort of covering. We do not share hats. But this hat has been shared. Has it, though? On this deeper level of meaning, are the hat-sharers really two different men, or does this very fact of sharing a hat tell us that on this level the captain and Leggatt are not two different men but two sides of the same man? Remember that before the hat was mentioned, Conrad keeps hinting at the close resemblance between the captain and Leggatt; they were almost the same age, had the same build, had come from the same background; they were almost like doubles or twins. What then is the meaning of all this? Why are the captain and the ship finally saved because the hat provides the steering mark?

THE SYMBOLISM OF THE WHOLE STORY

To attempt any reply to these questions we must now grapple with the symbolism not only of the hat but of the whole narrative. It will take us down to mysterious psychological depths. On this deepest level, the story can be interpreted as follows. Leggatt, who is impulsive and violent, who has been under arrest, who is now a fugitive, represents what some psychologists call "the shadow side" of the captain, that part of himself which he does not really know. Now this unknown shadow self does not belong (we quote the captain's own words) "to that ideal conception of one's own personality. . . ." And people who refuse to accept this shadow self, who idealize their own personalities, are dangerously lacking in self-knowledge. They may sooner or later find themselves at the mercy of this unknown past of the self, just because they have rejected it. But when the captain accepts, hides, and helps Leggatt, he is really accepting this other side of himself. The shared hat symbolizes the whole personality, which is whole because the shadow side has not been rejected, and therefore becomes the steering mark that enables the completed self to bring the ship out of danger, to assume successful command of officers and crew, to face life with confidence. This story then is not only a tale of an adventure at sea, nor even an account of how an act of kindness and generosity brought its own reward, but it is on its deepest level of meaning a parable of self-knowledge, an adventure of the soul.

Therefore it has to move slowly, just because it is so weighty with meaning. The beginning and ending, built up into wonderful seascapes, are superb, and are very typical of Conrad, who might be described as one of the greatest scene painters in modern fiction. The story is not perfect, from a technical point of view, if only because the arrival of Leggatt seems rather clumsily contrived. (Narrative that has symbolic depth is always harder to manage than straightforward one-level storytelling.) But in spite of a few flaws, *The Secret Sharer* is a little masterpiece of its kind, in which what had been a familiar old sea yarn is given wonderful color, excitement, fascinating depth of meaning, by Conrad's genius. He was a man who had had a hard life, from the time when, as a young Polish boy, he served his apprenticeship in the old sailing vessels, until the last few years of his life, when long-delayed recognition and adequate financial rewards came to him and eased the long struggle. He is at heart a tragic writer, who refuses to believe that everything can be made easy for everybody, that no effort is required, that satisfaction and even happiness can be laid on like hot and cold water. His years at sea taught him that men have to be prepared to meet the worst, and meet it honorably, with courage and self-reliance. The grim challenges, he feels, will always be there. So men must know themselves, the self in the shadow as well as the self in the sunlight. We must all be secret sharers.

Heroism in "The Secret Sharer"

Michael P. Jones

Michael P. Jones argues that Conrad's "The Secret Sharer" is a psychological journey into a fantasy world. Working in partnership with Leggatt, the captain tries to revive heroic achievement in a world of his own creation. Jones concludes that the captain achieves his heroic ethic by parting from Leggatt without sentiment. Michael P. Jones wrote his doctoral thesis, revised for publication, on Joseph Conrad while at Boston College.

Viewed simply with regard to its timing in Conrad's career, "The Secret Sharer" appears an eccentricity. Written nine years after *Lord Jim*, during the decade of *Nostromo* and *The Secret Agent* and almost simultaneously with the completion of *Under Western Eyes*, it is an adventure tale surrounded by Conrad's great political novels—seemingly a story rescued from Conrad's past. A number of critics speculate upon the conception of this tale, which [critic] Albert Guerard rightly calls the "most frankly psychological of Conrad's shorter works.". . .

The heroic journey in this story takes on the characteristics of a weird moral fable, a "doubles story," that defies most interpretive analysis, that maintains only the barest contact with the world of Marlow's England, with the demands of a critical audience. . . . In remaining true to his ideals Conrad extends his rebellion against the modern world, taking us into a grotesque and comic realm somewhere between fiction and fantasy, into a journey that twists and turns its way through the recesses of Conrad's heroic consciousness.

THE CAPTAIN CREATES A FANTASY UNIVERSE

Compared with the heroic journeys of the earlier adventure tales, that of the captain in "The Secret Sharer" occupies a

Excerpted from Michael P. Jones, *Conrad's Heroism: A Paradise Lost* (Ann Arbor, MI: UMI Research Press, 1985). Copyright © 1974, 1985 by Michael Pusey Jones. Reprinted by permission of the author. Endnotes in the original have been omitted in this reprint.

spatially diminished area, but at the same time one made larger by the captain and narrator. . . .

In "The Secret Sharer,". . . the godlike eye, which acknowledges a celestial audience, which proclaims the universe an arena for heroic ordeal, which takes the ordeal of initiation beyond the vision of the public world—this godlike eye belongs to the captain himself. . . . The external standards for heroic conduct are invented from the stage the captain sets up for himself on the deck of the ship. He clearly imagines his own moral universe in which he both legislates and performs the heroic ordeal. Moreover, it is apparent that to the captain, the physical journey of the ship is no more real or in any substantial way different from the metaphorical ways in which he treats it.

The idea of the story as a stage performance is central to the dramatic and narrative situations of "The Secret Sharer." The captain sees his professional duty as a performance before a celestial audience personified as spectators and critics, or perhaps as jurists. . . .

In this story, Conrad has abandoned his division between the narrator's fidelity to the heroic world and his responsibility to the "public." Self-conscious as he is, the captain never sees the necessity to justify to anyone the inventions of his heroic imagination. As a narrator, he is from the beginning removed from the social context in which Marlow appears, existing as the only voice and only as a voice in his storytelling, speaking from an unspecified time (apparently many years) after the event. We never see him through the eyes of a fictional public or with the perspective of a preliminary narrator. He appears, rather, only as a performer within and the inventor of his imaginative world. As a narrator he is only theoretically distinct from himself as an actor. Unlike Marlow, he is so engaged in the mind he describes and the incidents he relates that he never calls that mind or those incidents into question. . . .

THE CAPTAIN QUESTIONS HIS HEROISM IN HIS OWN IMAGINARY WORLD

In "The Secret Sharer" the captain is driven further into himself, into his imagination, wondering "how far I should turn out faithful to that ideal conception of one's own personality every man sets up for himself secretly." Like the equation between Jim and mankind, however, the one between the captain and "every man" is never really made. Like Jim, the captain needs his own world in which to perform his deeds—a remote area that serves as a refuge from the sordid places of courts of inquiry and cowardly masters. . . .

Still, in combination with the "spectator stars," the crew, in the mind of the captain, pose a threatening audience and jury and form a possibility of invasion into the captain's private heroic world. Shortly after the beginning of the story, the stars, rather than observing the captain, are described as "staring" at him, and the personified and private relationship with the ship (his "trusted friend") is broken by the "disturbing sounds" of footsteps and voices. The captain reads conspiracy even in the facial features of the chief mate, who approaches him "with an almost visible effect of collaboration on the part of his round eyes and frightful whiskers." He becomes a "stranger" to the ship and, as it were, to himself, as he fears he may be usurped from his position as the sole possessor of his command by the godlike presence in the world he has created in the privacy of his imagination.

THE ROLE OF LEGGATT IN THE CAPTAIN'S WORLD

When Leggatt becomes part of this tale, it is in a moral and psychological environment that requires for heroic conduct a reassertion of the ethics of heroism that were destroyed along with the pastoral world in *The Nigger of the "Narcissus"* and never regained in any convincing way in the Marlow stories. It is in the captain's relationship with Leggatt that the heroic community is revived. Through this partnership the captain may distinguish between a heroic community and everything that threatened such a community in *The Nigger of the "Narcissus"* and *Lord Jim:*

> The Sunday quietness of the ship was against us; the stillness of air and water around her was against us; the elements, the men were against us—everything was against us in our secret partnership; time itself—for this could not go on forever.

The abundant and insistent parallels between Leggatt and the captain are probably the best known feature of this story. Not only do these parallels include a repeated physical identification between the two men, as if they were identical twins, but also an analogy between their social and moral predicaments. Both men are young, and both are graduates of Conway; both are officers who attempt to assert their command in the face of real or imagined opposition from petty or cowardly men. Leggatt is a social outcast, running from public judgment in a situation analogous to the lonely drama of the captain, in which the "judges" belong to both the social and a celestial world. Often there is a silent communion between the two men, each appealing to the other as if they each perfectly understood, "as if our experiences had been as identical as our clothes." As these two men line up against each other, almost all the struggles of Conrad's imagination of the heroic are neatly and formulaically reviewed: the lonely initiation into manhood; the journey into the self; the problem of creating a heroic self outside of a fallen contemporary society; and the effort to reclaim the heroic community of the past. The communal and the private ideals behind Conrad's heroic imagination find expression in the relationship between Leggatt and the captain such that it becomes the epicenter of all the moral and dramatic energies of the story. Leggatt in this way is both man and metaphor, both a dramatic character and an imaginative vehicle for the values of the heroic imagination. . . .

If Leggatt is an avenging angel of Conrad's lost heroic world, it could stand to reason (the reason or rationale of the story, that is) that no one, besides the captain, ever "sees" him. When Captain Archbold of the *Sephora* comes aboard to meet his counterpart on the matter of Leggatt's escape, he tours the stateroom without detecting the murderer, who supposedly hides on the warning of Archbold's approach. In an even closer call, the steward goes into the captain's bathroom, where Leggatt is hiding, to hang a coat, but Leggatt escapes unseen: the explanation later given is that the steward put only his hand in the bathroom to hang up the coat. One of the characteristics of this story is that it is constantly creating incidents that raise the question of whether Leggatt "exists in the flesh." But beyond the energy expended in sustaining this ambiguity is the one indisputable fact that the world of the captain is dominated by a figure who for practical purposes is invisible to the rest of the crew, whose presence supplants the ship in the captain's fantasy of a personified and trusted friend, a figure whose spectral shadows seem to fill, beyond a mere physical existence, the captain's private world.

It is, of course, easy to see that, with this story's suggestion of an "alter-ego" for the captain, with the captain's seeming projections of guilt and paranoia into the character of Leggatt, with his repeated schizoid sense of himself as two people, "The Secret Sharer" confers psychological conditions on the world of heroic adventure that rarely if ever in Conrad's work suggest themselves to us in such clinical terms. The captain himself suspects he is nearly going mad, and in at least one specific instance confuses "inner" with "outer" realities, as he mistakes a knocking on the door with a knocking in his head. And then, too, we are offered the perspectives of his officers, who exchange knowing glances and tap their heads in gestures of amazed suspicion. But what strikes me as most interesting about these psychological overtones is not simply that the captain is mad, but rather the metaphorical identification between the captain's possible madness and the requirements of his heroic imagination. In that sense, the conditions of heroism in this story are connected to the conditions of Kurtz's heroism, whose godlike aspirations are identified with a kind of sublime madness. Still, the captain's madness in any mundane sense is somewhat beside the point. In a world where the metaphorical and the literal occupy the same plane of reality, heroism depends upon ignoring such distinctions— which the captain generally does.

But because the captain does refuse to sort out truth from artifice or madness from heroism, because he lacks the reflexive and self-questioning consciousness of Marlow, because he does seem to perform within an invented world, we as readers are permitted a perspective that in the end he neither possesses nor controls. The result is that the captain may be seen within a comic framework, but a framework which does not diminish him so much as it allows his freedom in one sense to become our freedom in another. Much of the fun of reading this story is not in trying to decide whether or not Leggatt exists but in observing how unable the captain is to consider such an issue. "Can it be," he asks himself in a way that characteristically neither confirms nor denies, "that he is not visible to other eyes than mine?" The fact that he is so incredulous over an obvious possibility implies that we may possess a freedom of imagination in observing his situation that he himself does not have. Yet he too is free—free to explore and dramatize his heroic imagination in a way that Marlow, with his dedication to the depressing truths of self-consciousness, could not. He is free even in his unselfconscious virtuosity in word play: "All's well so far," I whispered, "now you must vanish into the bath-room," he tells Leggatt. And later, when Archbold is in the stateroom, "My intelligent double had vanished. I had played my part." These represent just two instances in which "vanish" becomes a pun and in which the theatrical metaphor "played my part," comically enhances the captain's question-begging over Leggatt's physical existence.

THE QUESTION OF HEROIC ACHIEVEMENT

The very fact that this story may be read in a literary context where heroic achievement takes the form of self-delusion (as that of Fleming in *The Red Badge*[1] or the narrator in *The Nigger of the "Narcissus"*) alerts us to the possibilities and the limits of the captain's imagination. Yet the captain's unreliability as a narrator does not discredit his concept of heroism as the fantasies of Henry Fleming discredit his. That the captain is even more fantastic in his imagination than either Fleming or Jim—indeed, outrageously so—invites us to ask different questions about "The Secret Sharer." The question, "What is heroism?" is not necessary here; it becomes, rather, "Will the captain remain true to his vision of the heroic ideal and his imagination of the ideal self?" The weight of the drama correspondingly shifts from a quest for knowledge to a performance within an unquestioned code of ethics. And it is the performance, rather than the quest, that ultimately gives impetus to the drama.

In the relationship between the captain and Leggatt, the heroic imagination of Conrad is expressed in a fiction pretty close to fantasy. And this fantasy may be described as symbolic. Unfortunately, though, most interpretations of "The Secret Sharer" have made the story too tame, too Christian, too nineteenth-century. It is not a story about a young untried man whose ordeal facilitates his initiation into a social order and casts out the antisocial specter of his soul. The captain does become "initiated," but not into society, rather into an ideal. He is not ridding himself of demons but engineering a triumph of an abstract code of ethics which is asserted in the face of both social and universal opposition. Leggatt's act of murder is not crime but punish-

1. American novelist Stephen Crane's tale of an ordinary soldier's Civil War battle experience

ment against a fallen society; his escape is a flight from the modern world. The captain never doubts this, and Conrad himself was dismayed when a reviewer called Leggatt "a murderous ruffian." The way Leggatt speaks of his "crime" would draw applause from Marlow and Jim: "You don't suppose I am afraid of what can be done to me? Prison or gallows or whatever they may please. But you don't see me coming back to explain such things to an old fellow in a wig and twelve respectable tradesmen, do you? What can they know whether I am guilty or not—or of *what* I am guilty, either." In the context of the Marlow tales, it should be clear what significance judges, courtroom, and gallows have in Conrad's imagination of society as a conglomeration of arbitrary, antiheroic laws. It is only in the captain's relationship with Leggatt that Conrad envisions a society founded upon other laws, upon the principles of fidelity and service. For the first time in his career, Conrad looks into the depths of his mind and does not find darkness. Instead, he finds the lost heroic community, a unity within one mind, a communion with himself.

The captain in "The Secret Sharer" has declared war upon society—and what's more, he wins. As the "journey" approaches its conclusion, the comedy and the drama of the captain swell to splendid proportions. As the crew stare in horrified silence, the ship, approaching the shoals of Kohring, drifts in the captain's imagination to "the gate of everlasting night," the "very gate of Erebus."[2] (Is this so different from the mythical abyss in Wordsworth?[3]) Images of eternity and of a timeless land and seascape magnify and celebrate the captain's initiation, not into the social world, but into a communion with the asocial, nonhuman world of the universe and with the ship, which once again becomes his "friend":

> And I was alone with her. Nothing! no one in the world should stand now between us, throwing a shadow on the way of silent knowledge and mute affection, the perfect communion of a seaman with his first command.

We may hardly think the captain a bully or Leggatt a criminal in events which lead to such an affirmation of the heroic self.

Conrad, of course, has sacrificed the complexity of

2. in Greek mythology the dark region of the underworld through which the dead must pass before they reach Hades 3. British poet William

Marlow's relationship to the public world, as the "public" have become comparatively harmless cartoon characters. And disarming as the captain is, unlike Jim, Marlow, and Kurtz, he remains free of complicating realizations about the nature of heroism. When he "changes," it is only within the framework of his initially stated code of ethics, and we have to react to his limitations with mixed feelings. In one sense, they allow the captain's heroism to be untested by the forces of society or the "wilderness" which had made the struggles of Marlow and Kurtz so awesome. But in another, Conrad has taken us into another realm of fiction. Having sustained the delicate ambiguities of Leggatt's existence, Conrad seems to have created an unresolved dialectical relationship between romance and the public world and has combined the external journey of nineteenth-century adventure fiction with the Wordsworthian inner journey into the self. The result is spontaneous and liberating.

THE CAPTAIN PUT TO THE TEST

Because we may read this story in the context of the earlier tales, Conrad's presence in "The Secret Sharer" is larger, and in a subtle, almost vapid way, more pervasive than that of the captain. There is a poignancy in the captain's reaction to Leggatt's decision to leave the ship, which takes us back to and at the same time beyond Conrad's elegiac celebrations of a lost paradise in the earlier novels. The captain protests that Leggatt must not leave; but Leggatt insists, with characteristic ellipses, that indeed he will, saying finally, "You have understood thoroughly. Didn't you?" For the captain, and in a crucial way for Conrad, this becomes a revelation: "I felt suddenly ashamed of myself. I may say truly that I understood—and my hesitation in letting that man swim away from my ship's side had been a mere sham sentiment, a sort of cowardice." The captain's confession of cowardice and profession of faith in his friendship with Leggatt gives the heroic ethic a kind of living, spiritual presence in his imagination of the hero in the modern world. It is a response that supersedes mere nostalgia. The captain will never "lose" Leggatt even in saying farewell to him; and he certainly will not try to hold on to him in a way that is melancholy or self-indulgently sentimental. Time, we recall from a passage I quoted earlier, is against their secret partnership, but the captain overcomes even the degeneration of time by the end of the story.

The last paragraph of "The Secret Sharer" also takes us beyond our earlier objections to Conrad's sentimentality and forced allegorizing, while he maintains his allegiance to the heroic ethic and sustains the parallels between Leggatt and the captain, asserting the triumph of the heroic self:

> Walking to the taffrail, I was in time to make out, on the very edge of a darkness thrown by a towering black mass like the very gateway of Erebus—yes, I was in time to catch an evanescent glimpse of my white hat left behind to mark the spot where the secret sharer of my cabin and of my thoughts, as though he were my second self, had lowered himself into the water to take his punishment: a free man, a proud swimmer striking out for a new destiny.

Surely we must applaud the captain, as he indeed invites us to do throughout the story. Possibly it is the brilliance of focusing his sentimentality on the small white cap, rather than Leggatt himself, that saves the passage from the pathos of the conclusion of *The Nigger of the "Narcissus."* Rather than a madman, the captain sounds like a hero in triumph, and his triumph seems to justify and ameliorate his handling of the crew. The story in the end sounds so right, the sentiments so poised, that "The Secret Sharer" must indeed win us over to the heroic ethic that the Marlow tales had lost.

Conrad, the Sea, and "The Secret Sharer"

Morton Dauwen Zabel

Morton Dauwen Zabel argues that "The Secret Sharer" is a pivotal piece in Conrad's work. Zabel shows that Conrad has mastered the art of the modern sea story, that Conrad's sea experience has shaped his philosophy and imagination, and that "The Secret Sharer" succinctly states Conrad's major moral theme and illustrates his art of storytelling. The story typifies Conrad's overall method of using the sea as a device to test the individual and reality. Morton Dauwen Zabel was a teacher and critic. He is the author of *Craft and Character* and the editor of the Viking *Portable Conrad.*

If Conrad remains, after what is now more than half a century, the unchallenged master among English writers of sea tales, his claim to the title may be said to have been defined in the three stories collected in the present volume ["Typhoon," "The Secret Sharer" and *The Shadow-Line*] and in two others, "Youth" and *The Nigger of the "Narcissus."* The sea and its life of course figure in a large number of his other tales; it is a recurring presence from his first book to his last. . . .

CONRAD MASTERED THE ART OF THE SEA STORY

A "tale of the sea" requires, if the term is to have accurate or specific value, a certain definition. It must involve a way of life and conduct, an ethic of dedication and purpose, an actuality of experience and vocation. . . . Poets and allegorists, epic scribes and chroniclers, several eminent novelists on occasion, one notable modern dramatist, minor and popular writers before and after Conrad almost without number, have shaped a long tradition of sea literature and made that tradition more conspicuous in English than in any other modern literature. . . . Yet by one of the curious chances that play their

Excerpted from Morton Dauwen Zabel, introduction to *The Shadow-Line and Two Other Tales*, by Joseph Conrad, edited and with an introduction by Morton Dauwen Zabel (New York: Doubleday, 1959). Copyright © 1959 by Morton Dauwen Zabel.

part in the fortunes of literature, it was left to the Polish Conrad, soon after his first appearance as an English novelist in 1895, to raise that order of English narrative to a rank of serious and fully responsible art it had hardly achieved before his arrival and has scarcely shown with equal force since. . . .

It may be said with equal assurance today that Conrad is the English master of the sea story, and that his mastery is most fully realized, is given its most concentrated expression and authority, in *The Nigger*, "Youth," "Typhoon," "The Secret Sharer," and *The Shadow-Line.*

The title was to give him serious doubts and some uneasy feeling in his later years, when he saw the fame of his "sea stuff" threatening to crowd out his other claims as a novelist in the minds of his readers and critics. He was fully aware of the romantic and superficial appeal of his *métier*,[1] and of the popular uses to which his material had been put by the facile entertainers of his day. It became his hope, when he finally arrived at the honors of a collected edition of his books, "to get freed from that infernal tail of ships and that obsession with my sea life" which even his best-intentioned publishers and critics had fixed on to promote his reputation. "After all, I may have been a seaman, but I am a writer of prose," he argued on one of these occasions. "Indeed, the nature of my writing runs the risk of being obscured by the nature of my material." "I admit it is natural," he allowed, but "such headings as 'Spinner of sea yarns—master mariner—seaman writer,'" came to rankle increasingly as he saw the celebrity for which he had waited during two anxious decades mount and the stricter ambition of his art become lost on many of his admirers. "You know how the public mind fastens on externals, on mere facts, such for instance as ships and voyages, without paying any attention to any deeper significance they may have," he pled to one of his interpreters, and to another: "A work of art is very seldom limited to one exclusive meaning and not necessarily tending to a definite conclusion. And this for the reason that the nearer it approaches art, the more it acquires a symbolic character.". . .

THE SEA SHAPES CONRAD'S OUTLOOK

Yet there is no question that the sea was a supreme experience in his life; that it gave him a school of experience more

---

1. specialty; the work in which he excelled

important to him as a character and moral dramatist than any other he had known; that he viewed his relationship to it as something like a personal trust and calling; and that it gave him not only his richest single fund of material but the most powerful symbol of his art. Not even the inheritance of heroism, idealism, and tragedy that had come to him by his birth in Poland was to serve him so effectively in his practical and imaginative life. . . .

It was in the sea and its ships that he found the sense of community, dedication, and responsibility that had failed him in Poland and France, and though his relations with it were eventually to show all the complexity of emotion and conflict of intelligence that could be expected in a man of Conrad's nature, his feeling of identification with its life and "passion" remained with him to the end. . . .

The sea was similarly bound to appeal to him—as it has appealed to men of every age—in its aspects of primary or elemental force, its mindless oblivion and inhuman power: "too great, too mighty for common virtues," "faithful to no race after the manner of the kindly earth," with "no compassion, no faith, no law, no memory," no response to human need or vanity: an expression not only of the justice but of the indifference of nature. It is as such a presence that it figures in some of his most memorable passages—the voyage of the *Patna* in *Lord Jim;* the storm scenes of *The Nigger* and "Typhoon"; the great night scene of the silver-laden lighter on the Golfo Placido in *Nostromo;* the sinister calms that enclose the vessels in "The Secret Sharer" and *The Shadow-Line.* These are passages that deserve a place among the classic pictures of the sea in any age—*Odyssey, The Tempest, Moby Dick. . . .*

In the sea Conrad found in inseparable union the forces of nature and action that best served his temper and imagination, a mode of experience in which fact and fantasy met on a common and necessary ground:

> I knew it capable of betraying the generous ardour of youth as implacably as, indifferent to evil and good, it would have betrayed the basest greed or the noblest heroism. My conception of its magnanimous greatness was gone. . . . Open to all and faithful to none, it exercises its fascination for the undoing of the best. To love it is not well. It knows no bond of plighted troth, no fidelity to misfortune, to long companionship, to long devotion. The promise it holds out perpetually is very great; but the only secret of its possession is strength,

strength—the jealous, sleepless strength of a man guarding a coveted treasure within his gates.

The eloquence of the phrasing, the personal pathos and metaphor, the emphasis on *anima* [2]—none of these cancels the sense of something that was more important to the writer who put them to dramatic and allegoric use in his tales: his practiced knowledge of the sea as a test of mind and character. That knowledge remains basic to all of Conrad's more serious and convincing uses of the sea in his books; and none of his protests against the popular fame the sea brought him can deny its value to him as the central instrument of his moral imagination and the most powerful single factor—reality or symbol—in his creative achievement.

"Typhoon," "The Secret Sharer," and *The Shadow-Line* . . . may be taken as a trilogy on their common subject. They show in fact a progression in their treatment of it. Each turns on a crisis of shock, challenge, or initiation. . . . "If there is to be any classification by subjects," Conrad said of these stories, "I have done two Storm-pieces in *The Nigger of the 'Narcissus'* and in 'Typhoon'; and two Calm-pieces: 'The Secret Sharer' and *The Shadow-Line*." Storm at its wildest and deadliest plays its part in "Typhoon," calm in its most sinister and spectral malignity in *The Shadow-Line;* while another quiescence [3] of sea and sky, a trance of stillness between foul weather and fair, acts its role in the drama of "The Secret Sharer." The great storms of *The Nigger* and "Typhoon" engulf the ships in those tales with all the fury of conscious intention and hostility in the elements. . . .

THE THEME OF THE OTHER SELF

"The Secret Sharer" shows the other and more salient side of Conrad's mind and art. The story, written at a time of acute preoccupation when he had both *Under Western Eyes* and *Chance* on his hands, both defying completion, is perhaps of all his tales the one most consciously written as an emblem or epigram of his essential moral subject. Its theme had worked in his tales from the beginning. It had become overt in "Heart of Darkness," exhaustive in *Lord Jim*, essential in *Nostromo;* and it was presently to arrive at further extension in *Under Western Eyes*. The drama of the other self, whether

---

2. an inner feminine nature   3. quietness; inaction

the Platonic ego, the unrecognized unconscious, or the compulsive identity making its claim on the precarious and untested conscience, had given focus to the novels from the time of Almayer and Willems; it had clearly laid an obsessive claim on Conrad's imagination as he progressed more deeply into his study of human fate and character. "The Secret Sharer" not only gives a name to the subject; it brings it to its most concise allegoric expression, which means also to something resembling a mythic condition. Division, duplicity, deception, the fated duality of "self and soul," are radical throughout Conrad's drama; and the experiences that are compelled by them—recognition, sympathy, identification, self-knowledge—become their necessary cognates in all his major tales.

The story hinges on the precarious moment in the seaman's life when he takes his first command—when he passes at a stroke from the shared life of a crew to the responsible isolation of authority. Uneasy in his office; suddenly sensing for the first time the peril of leaving the land for the solitary life of a ship; surrounded by the skeptical suspicion of his crew; acutely aware of his untested authority, the young captain enters on his command as if exposed to an insecurity he has never before felt in his life. Alone on his deck in the night watch which he has broken the rule of the ship in keeping, he finds himself uneasily vulnerable to everything his exposure implies—self-doubt, stirrings of conscience, a sense of solitude and estrangement. And there it is, in the calm of night and out of the darkened water, that there comes to him the naked man who makes his appeal to his sympathy—Leggatt the murderer. Leggatt has killed a man, has done so for good reason yet against the law of men and ships; and has taken to the sea in flight from an impersonal justice: "a fugitive and a vagabond on the earth, with no brand of the curse on his sane forehead to stay a slaying hand." By an involuntary instinct that defies the law of his ship and office, the captain takes him aboard; condones his crime; conceals him in his cabin, gives him his own sleeping-suit to wear and his berth to lie in; finds himself sharing Leggatt's secret existence while denying it to the crew and the world. Another self has come to live in the masked rectitude of his life. "I was somewhat of a stranger to myself," the captain had felt when he took charge of his boat and its hostile crew; "I wondered how far I should turn out faithful to that ideal conception of one's own personality every man sets up for himself secretly." It is Leggatt, coming out of sea and darkness like a stealthy messenger from the unknown, who gives him his chance to find out.

The test Leggatt has met and acted on now becomes a test for the captain. He finds himself, for the first time, living a double life in which his authority must conceal the deception that defies and outlaws it. He carries through his deception of the crew; and when the time comes to give Leggatt his chance to return, naked once more, to the water, strike out for land, and "take his punishment" as "a free man, a proud swimmer striking out for a new destiny," he steers his ship so close to the rocky headland of Koh-ring that he risks as if by necessity its destruction. But not before he has snatched off his hat, his headpiece, and rammed it on Leggatt's head for protection against the sun that will beat mercilessly on him: only to find, as the keel nears the rocks, that the hat floats on the water and gives him a marker by which he can steer himself and his ship to safety.

The night, the silent sea, the naked swimmer, the concealment, the gift of the sleeping-suit, garb of the unconscious life, the lie enacted to the crew and the captain of the *Sephora*, the return of the fugitive to the sea, the hat that becomes a guide to steer by—the parts these play in the fable are evident. Conrad's intention in writing the tale becomes not only overt but explicit. The story risks offending against itself by making its secret too plain, its hero too aware of what is happening to him in his conspiracy with his other self. It is in the ordeals of Kurtz and Marlow, Lord Jim and Razumov, Decoud and Nostromo, that Conrad's drama of the alter ego takes on the richer force of psychic confusion and duplicity. He wrote "The Secret Sharer" as if to give an axiomatic[4] statement of his central theme. Even so, the statement becomes something more than axiomatic. The spell of its atmosphere and imagery, the economy of action and event, the sustaining hint of meanings beyond the captain's conscious sense of collusion in guilt and secrecy, combine to make "The Secret Sharer" a fable that becomes focal not only in Conrad's own work but to an essential part of modern writing generally. It shows the conscious design and pregnant suggestiveness of archetypal fiction. . . .

4. self-evident

THE SEA AS A MEASURE OF REALITY

"Both men and ships live in an unstable element," Conrad said in *The Mirror of the Sea.* That instability is the sphere and condition of his dramas, whether of life at sea or life in the world. The tests he met, the truths he learned, during his sailing years became the realities to which he addressed himself in his art. They are realities that assume many forms of peril, risk, and evil in his tales: now intimate or secret, now public, social, or historical, they rise as challenges to character and survival for men in every walk of life. It was in his tales of ships and seamen that Conrad brought them to some of the most effective and accurate expressions he ever arrived at, and it is their workings there that have made these stories classic of their kind—images in which "the sea interpenetrates with life" and becomes "a factor in the problem of existence."

CHAPTER 3

Conrad's Early Novels, 1897–1900

The Significance of Character in *The Nigger of the 'Narcissus'*

Maxine Greene

Maxine Greene analyzes ship life on the *Narcissus*, showing how the character of crew members is revealed during a storm. The central character, James Wait, has a dangerous effect on the crew because his illusions "infect" them, cause unrest, and weaken their resolve. By contrast, the experienced seaman, old Singleton, stays the helm and steers the ship during the storm. Greene maintains that Conrad believed in the necessity of Singleton's kind of commitment, honor, and discipline, qualities considered outmoded in Conrad's time. Maxine Greene taught at New York University, the Teachers College of Columbia University, and the University of Illinois. She is the author of several books on education.

The *Narcissus* is a sailing ship, and when we meet her she is moored in tropical waters, about to sail. It is, at first, as if we are seeing her across great distances, under an utterly blank sky. There are shadowy figures below her decks, a group of faceless creatures, "turning upon itself with the motion of a scrimmage" in a swirl of tobacco smoke. Then, suddenly, we are near them, with them, indeed in their midst. We can define individuals now, faces: the bearded, serene old man propped against the bowsprit, reading like "a learned and savage patriarch"; the street-boy's face bent over a length of rope; the little, red-faced, boiling Irishman. In another moment, we discern the roving, beady eyes of Donkin, shirtless, in a filthy, ragged suit; and, at last, after the quiet routine of the muster, there is the towering figure of James Wait rising over the rail. Like the crew, we wonder at his "tormented, flattened face," emerging from the darkness and

Excerpted from Maxine Greene, introduction to *The Nigger of the "Narcissus,"* by Joseph Conrad (New York: Doubleday, 1914).

teetering on the edge of something we are not sure of, something we are strangely afraid to see.

We are in the universe of *The Nigger of the Narcissus*; and, land-bound though we may be, it is our universe as well, viewed in a mirror that elongates and expands. The business of literature, after all, is not to reflect but to create a semblance of reality; and this semblance, this story, reveals to us beliefs and sentiments we scarcely knew we possessed, things hidden below the surface of the everyday. A simple reproduction could not do this, just as a photograph cannot. It takes a work of art shaped by a human being, by a vital organism who perceives "reality" in ways determined by his unique experience, his temperament, the language available to him, the feelings and responses he has developed in a lifetime.

THE WORLD OF CONRAD'S CREATION

The "reality" that Joseph Conrad perceived was, like the head of James Wait, "vigorously modeled into deep shadows and shining lights." His world was a haunted one, with mystery in its depths. He could tell about it best if he symbolized—or represented—it in the most extreme and desperate kinds of situations. As he writes in the *Preface*, he wished to appeal "to that part of our being which is not dependent on wisdom" and to do so by making us hear, feel, and, "before all," to *see*.

The extreme situations he chose were usually those involving people living in the abandoned places of the earth: the jungles, tropical islands, and, most often, in some ship, some "fragment detached from the earth," moving among "abysses of sky and sea." Conrad could make such choices because he had spent much of his life in just such isolated places, and he could communicate their haunting strangeness because he had been a stranger so often, and so often alone. . . .

He was a handsome man, a commanding man, not only a sea captain, but, as his biographer says, a "sea-dreamer" as well. He watched and pondered the behavior of men when they were far from civilization, from the laws, obligations, and social conventions that guide us and give us support. He moved among men who had to cope with the primitive and the violent both in the outside world and in their own natures, and to do so without help. He saw them, therefore, thrown back upon themselves, tested to the limit by the worthy and unworthy causes they espoused, revealing themselves in their heroism or cowardice in a world where the dangerous and unknowable, like x-ray beams, made visible the bare bones of their plight. . . .

The Nigger of the Narcissus was published in 1897, soon after Conrad launched his literary struggle; and we can find in it multiple echoes of his somber dreams. We can discern, too, the shapes of all his future themes, as we probe with him into the vigorous actuality of life on the precarious seas.

If we knew nothing about the author, we would guess immediately that the *Narcissus* and its crew have been formed from firsthand experience, snatched "from the remorseless rush of time." Only a man who had sailed under all sorts of conditions, with all sorts of shipmates, could describe in such detail that exacting, beautiful sea boat, the etiquette of the forecastle with its glaring lamps and tiers of bunks, the galley and poop and mainmast—the oblique leap, with reefed sails, at the waves. A weakness in the story is reputedly the shift of narrative point of view, when the narrator, beginning in the third person, abruptly changes to first person and speaks as a member of the crew. This may be a technical flaw; but the shift seems somehow inevitable in the context of the book, particularly when we feel the sense of intimate involvement in the careless and impassioned discussions of the crew, in the circle of the watches, in the life on board on calm days—and before the inconceivable challenge of the storm.

THE CREW OF THE *NARCISSUS*

Belfast, old Singleton, Charlie, Archie, and the rest are diverse individuals of a range of ages and backgrounds. No one of them is entirely good or entirely evil: no one of them is entirely blind, and no one sees it all. They compose "a good crowd" and, at once, "a crazy crowd of tinkers"; they function with different degrees of effectiveness under the grave Olympian leadership of Captain Allistoun and the innocuous gruffness of Mr. Baker, the "model first mate."

Their voyage would be an ordinary one, for all its perils, if it were not for James Wait, who appears so dramatically when the muster is done, who "fascinated us," overshadowed and tainted everyone who came in contact with him. He is "our nigger"; but it should be understood that the term, for all the overtones that Jimmy himself detected, did not carry the scorn and opprobrium for Conrad that it carries for contemporary Americans with their painful memories of

STEADFAST SINGLETON

In the turmoil of the storm, many excited crewmen are reduced to aimless activities. The following excerpt from The Nigger of the 'Narcissus' *shows that experienced old Singleton, by contrast, stood firmly at the wheel.*

Through the clear sunshine, over the flashing turmoil and uproar of the seas, the ship ran blindly, dishevelled and head-long, as if fleeing for her life; and on the poop we spun, we tot-tered about, distracted and noisy. We all spoke at once in a thin babble; we had the aspect of invalids and the gestures of maniacs. Eyes shone, large and haggard, in smiling, meagre faces that seemed to have been dusted over with powdered chalk. We stamped, clapped our hands, feeling ready to jump and do anything; but in reality hardly able to keep on our feet. Captain Allistoun, hard and slim, gesticulated madly from the poop at Mr. Baker: "Steady these fore-yards! Steady them the best you can!" On the main deck, men excited by his cries, splashed, dashing aimlessly here and there with the foam swirling up to their waist. Apart, far aft, and alone by the helm, old Singleton had deliberately tucked his white beard under the top button of his glistening coat. Swaying upon the din and tumult of the seas, with the whole battered length of the ship launched forward in a rolling rush before his steady old eyes, he stood rigidly still, forgotten by all, and with an attentive face. In front of his erect figure only the two arms moved crosswise with a swift and sudden readiness, to check or urge again the rapid stir of circling spokes. He steered with care.

Joseph Conrad, *The Nigger of the 'Narcissus,'* with a new introduction by Maxine Green. New York: Collier Books, 1962.

prejudice and slavery. Meanings are determined by the con-text, connotations vary with the occasions on which words are used. Even as the rough language of seamen can be accepted because of the circumstances of their lives, so must the word "nigger" be accepted as it refers to James Wait, in his great dignity and scorn, and with his tragic gestures of denial, which make him the crucial center of this tale.

But what do James Wait's gestures mean? Why does he arouse such love and such unrest among the men? What explains his odd and suspect friendship with Donkin? Why does his very presence make the crew members civilized, decadent, and, at once, so afraid?

On the surface, we see a person immobilized by suffering, whether that suffering is feigned or unfeigned; and we watch his shipmates respond to him with love, irritation, concern. But we also sense the chill and gloom that exude from the sick man; we feel it settling over the ship; and we become aware that Wait is a carrier of illusions, even of fraud.

For Conrad, the illusion that verges on mendacity, on what he calls "audacious lies," is as threatening an element as the dark sea. It is not only harmful to the man who carries it and lives by it; in some manner, it is contagious and infects others, especially when the others are superstitious and uninformed. Like a disease, it works through their fundamental weakness and thrusts them into an ambiguous world, where they exist as reduced creatures, lacking honor, lacking even dignity. They begin to resemble, in a word, the irresponsible Donkin, who not only shirks his jobs, but claims special privileges as one of the oppressed.

There are ways, of course, of combating such infection; and Conrad shows us that there is a potent medicine in doing the jobs that have to be done. Duty, discipline, all the postures and attitudes required for running a good ship can become a defense against self-serving sickness, against the grim preoccupations that make strong men weak and soft. Responsible team work, too, serves as a barrier against destructive fears; and we find this out when we experience the storm that batters the ship for hour upon hour, when the crew members are face to face with the threat of actual death.

A STORM TESTS THE CREW

Conrad is famous for his descriptions of storms, in this story, as in *Typhoon;* these descriptions, in fact, help give him a reputation as a writer of superb adventure yarns, and in some of its dimensions, this story is one of these. But the storm is far more than adventure here; it is a means of testing the crew, of displaying the strengths and weaknesses of the sailors when they are being buffeted from without and within. Captain Allistoun remains stern and immovable in his command, as the seamen tie themselves together in protection against the heaving sea. Young Charley is fastened to a ringbolt "with someone's long muffler"; and when he weeps, his neighbors cover him and encircle him in their arms. The cook preaches; Mr. Baker encourages; and, throughout the entire squall, old Singleton stands "rigidly still" at the helm and steers the ship with care. Singleton has lived long and seen much; he *knows,* simple and childish though he may be. Resigned, accepting, he is the opposite of the complaining Donkin: old Singleton, knowing too much to ask questions, stays on the job and steers.

The other crew members, sickened and disrupted, have not learned what he has learned. James Wait, in his retreat, keeps tempting them with illusions; they crowd before his open door and watch. We can understand; and we collaborate, for a time, with the crew. We want to foster the illusion, we want to keep it alive. In the central scene of the rescue (that repetition of the Jonah tale), we are like the seamen scraping at the nail-strewn floor; we love and hate at once. "And we hated him because of the suspicion, we detested him because of the doubt. We could not scorn him safely—neither could we pity him without risk to our dignity. So we hated him and passed him carefully hand to hand." Reading, we feel a kindred conflict; because we know that to live in helpless panic like Wait's is to give up all hope of maturity, of honor. If we are fortunate, we find ourselves refusing to make such a sacrifice. And we heed, without first realizing it, a moral lesson that is never spelled out, an insight that is never given didactic form. In our time, especially, it is an insight we desperately need.

CONRAD IN RELATION TO OTHER WRITERS

The lesson speaks of commitment and devotion to ideal standards, norms outmoded by the time of Conrad's death in 1924, but for all that, urgently necessary in our unpredictable world. It was a simple matter, in a newly scientific era, to scorn the old-fashioned codes of honor and of discipline; freedom was the all-important value, along with the right to protest, to revolt. Our liberties, surely, are still important; but, at a moment when talk and tests of bombs immobilize and panic us, we need more than a commitment to freedom if we are to lead meaningful lives.

Conrad's work suggests that we must find a way of confronting the certainties as well as the uncertainties in life; it tells us that we must find an honorable mode of living with them. The irresponsibility of denial and withdrawal can be as evil, as disruptive in our lives as it is on the decks of the *Narcissus.* It can only be surmounted if we remain strong and dedicated, if we hold on to our integrity, if we cling to each other when the storms come and pull on the ropes together when they pass. Our work, writes Conrad, must be "hard and unceasing"; this means, in part, that we commit ourselves to our jobs of work, that we make our lives significant by continuing to make things, to create, to order, to learn. The alternative, as some of us already know, is inertia and apathy; and with these goes meaninglessness, which means defeat.

It is not surprising that Conrad has achieved a contemporary popularity greater than the popularity he finally achieved before the first World War. It is not surprising that *Narcissus* suggests to us, not simply the fatal self-concern which isolates a man like Wait, but the dangers of staring at our own reflections, of remaining crouched and immobile instead of entering community life and pursuing human goals. We are ready for such self-examination by means of art; we need to be involved.

THE NOVEL'S INSIGHTS

When Conrad began writing, this was not so. It was fashionable, at the turn of the century, to write from a detached vantage point or with a moralistic, didactic attitude. Conrad learned much from men like Gustave Flaubert, who worked for impersonality and for the objectivity that could be secured only if the precise words were found. He learned from Henry James, with his oblique approach to human relations, his precise analyses of character. And, as a Slav himself, he learned from Russian writers like Dostoievski, who probed deeply to discover how men might become Christlike, how they might learn truly to love. He antagonized those concerned with "art for art's sake"; he alienated those who thought art should "improve." He found his own road, the road to an art form as deliberately shaped as Flaubert's and as palpitant with moral fervor as Dostoievski's; but it was his own kind of art, a "sea-dreamer's" art, and it flowed forward into a later day.

André Gide read him and praised him; Thomas Mann spoke of him as an exemplary artist; Scott Fitzgerald studied his works. *The Nigger of the Narcissus* does not need their recommendation, however; it might have been written for us yesterday or even today. Voyaging by means of it, moving through the vacancies from Bombay Harbor to the "stony shores" of the Thames, we are likely to find something waiting for us when we arrive in port; it may be a fresh vision of ourselves.

The Significance of the Crew in *The Nigger of the 'Narcissus'*

James E. Miller Jr.

James E. Miller Jr. argues that the crew of the *Narcissus* is the focal point around which Conrad builds his theme, symbols, structure, and style. Miller identifies two sets of conflicting symbols— Wait versus the sea and Donkin versus Singleton— that vie for the crew's allegiance. Miller shows the crew evolving from ignorant disarray, to unity based on a lie, to true unity—a solid "knot" of sailors in the image of Singleton, who is wise about the meaning of life and death. James E. Miller Jr. has taught at the University of Michigan, the University of Nebraska, and the University of Chicago. In addition to this analysis of Conrad, his published work includes studies of American authors F. Scott Fitzgerald, Walt Whitman, and Herman Melville. He is the author of *Critical Guide to "Leaves of Grass"* and *Fictional Techniques of F. Scott Fitzgerald.*

I wish to support the thesis that the subject of *Nigger* may be defined in somewhat precise terms, and, furthermore, that the techniques and structure embodying and setting forth that subject are of such a quality as to make the novel worthy of consideration as a classic, perhaps minor but in no sense negligible. . . .

It is the crew, collectively, that occupies the center of the novel. But Conrad is not concerned with everything that happens to the crew on board the *Narcissus* (such a catalogue of events, if not impossible, would surely not make a novel); more precisely, he is concerned with tracing a change that takes place in the crew: in general terms, the crew passes from ignorance to knowledge about life and about death; as a

Excerpted from James E. Miller, "*The Nigger of the 'Narcissus'*: A Reexamination," *PMLA* 66 (1951), pp. 911–18. Reprinted by permission of the Modern Language Association of America and the author.

result, and more specifically, the transition in the crew is from diversity to solidarity. It is on this change that Conrad focuses our attention, and it is within the terms of this change that he constructs his symbols, and it is the drama of this change that *is* the structure of the novel. A brief glance at the opening and close of *Nigger* bears out the central importance of this transition. As the novel opens, it is night, and our attention is directed to the forecastle: "A hum of voices was heard there, while port and starboard, in the illuminated doorways, silhouettes of moving men appeared for a moment, very black, without relief, like figures cut out of sheet tin." It is, indeed, as a "clash of voices and cries" that the crew, a diverse group of many nationalities, first appears to us. In the final pages of the novel, one striking sentence pictures the crew for us in very different terms: "The dark knot of seamen drifted in sunshine." The crew has, in the progress of the novel, passed out of the darkness of ignorance into the light of wisdom; it has changed from clashing diversity into the peaceful solidarity of a "knot." And the closing lines of the novel suggest the significance of the experience the crew has undergone: "Haven't we, together and upon the immortal sea, wrung out a meaning from our sinful lives?"

THE FOUR MAJOR SYMBOLS

To discover this meaning is to discover the knowledge which the crew gained on its voyage on the *Narcissus*. Perhaps the knowledge can best be explained in terms of the dominant symbols of the book (at the risk, of course, of oversimplification): James Wait and the sea, as symbols of death and life; Singleton and Donkin, as symbols of opposed attitudes toward death and life. The significance that James Wait is to have in the novel and the attitude of the crew toward him as symbol are shadowed forth in the opening chapter, in a brief scene constructed around the ambiguity of Wait's name:

> The distinct and motionless group stirred, broke up, began to move forward. "Wait!" cried a deep, ringing voice.
> All stood still.

The electrifying command of the voice and name instil in the crew that uneasiness with which it is to be plagued throughout the book. The ambiguity becomes reality in the second chapter, when the crew comes to know Wait for what he is, death in disguise: "A black mist emanated from him; a subtle and dismal influence; a something cold and gloomy that floated out and settled on all the faces like a mourning veil."

As the crew is to take its lesson of death from James Wait, so it is to take its lesson of life from the sea. The mysterious, enigmatical, and immortal sea comes to violent life in the third chapter; in a very real sense, it *becomes* life for the moment and gives the crew a vision of itself that is the sum of wisdom:

> On men reprieved by its disdainful mercy, the immortal sea confers in its justice the full privilige of desired unrest. Through the perfect wisdom of its grace they are not permitted to meditate at ease upon the complicated and acrid savour of existence. They must without pause justify their life to the eternal pity that commands toil to be hard and unceasing, from sunrise to sunset, from sunset to sunrise; till the weary succession of nights and days tainted by the obstinate clamour of sages, demanding bliss and an empty heaven, is redeemed at last by the vast silence of pain and labour, by the dumb fear and the dumb courage of men obscure, forgetful, and enduring.

Closely related to these symbols are Donkin and Singleton, who represent opposed attitudes toward death and life, attitudes which vie with each other to dominate the crew. Donkin is introduced to us as "the man that cannot steer, that cannot splice, that dodges the work on dark nights . . . the man who curses the sea while the others work. . . . [He] knows nothing of courage, of endurance, and of the unexpressed faith, of the unspoken loyalty that knits together a ship's company." Donkin thus becomes ignorance personified, just as old Singleton is "the incarnation of barbarian wisdom." Unfortunately, Singleton is the last of an unremembered, unsung race: "The men who could understand his silence were gone—those men who knew how to exist beyond the pale of life and within sight of eternity. They had been strong, as those are strong who know neither doubts nor hopes."

Donkin and Singleton (the names themselves are suggestive: Donkin connotes that stupidest of animals, while Singleton connotes integrity, solidarity) are the two poles between which the crew vacillates. Donkin in his sneaking attitude toward death (James Wait) and his cowardly attitude toward life (the sea), represents the ultimate in that ignorance from which the crew eventually passes to the primitive wisdom of Singleton, as exhibited in the contrasting courageous acceptance of death and life for what they are. Thus Conrad brings back to life the race of men,

Singleton's comrades, which he at first told us was extinct, for the men of the *Narcissus* at the end of its voyage do know "toil, privation, violence, debauchery—but [know] not fear, and [have] no desire of spite in their hearts."

And what is this primitive wisdom which the crew possesses at the end of its voyage? It is important first to see what it is not: "He [James Wait] was demoralising. Through him we were becoming highly humanised, tender, complex, excessively decadent: we understood the subtlety of his fear, sympathised with all his repulsions, shrinkings, evasions, delusions—as though we had been overcivilised, and rotten, and without any knowledge of the meaning of life." This "knowledge of the meaning of life" is not a sophisticated, complex, highly civilized or civilizing (in the usual sense) knowledge; it is, rather, a basic insight into fundamental, primitive truths. It is, first, a view of life which results not so much in an understanding as in an attitude of acceptance. Life *is* toil, *is* privation, *is* violence, as only the sea can prove; and it is not man's place to doubt or shrink from these hard facts of life, any more than it is his place to doubt or shrink from the mysterious sea. He must acknowledge and accept them with courage. But the wisdom is also a wisdom of death. It is this insight that Singleton has in the midst of the voyage of the *Narcissus:* "He looked upon the immortal sea with the awakened and groping perception of its heartless might; he saw it unchanged, black and foaming under the eternal scrutiny of the stars; he heard its impatient voice calling for him out of a pitiless vastness full of unrest, of turmoil, and of terror. He looked far upon it, and he saw an immensity tormented and blind, moaning and furious, that claimed all the days of his tenacious life, and, when life was over, would claim the worn-out body of its slave." Singleton's wisdom has been completed; his vision of life has been extended to a vision of death, death as inexplicable, inevitable, to be accepted with the same courage with which life has been accepted. This primitive wisdom of life and death, which the crew is to possess by the end of the voyage, is, as Conrad tells us in his preface, the source of solidarity, "the solidarity in mysterious origin, in toil, in joy, in hope, in uncertain fate, which binds men to each other and all mankind to the visible world." The "knot" which binds the crew at the end of *Nigger* is indeed, a sailor's knot, tied with a sailor's wisdom.

THE DRAMATIC STRUCTURE

The structure of *Nigger* is essentially dramatic. Suspense is achieved through the juxtaposition of two probabilities: the one probability is that the crew will turn to Singleton, achieve his wisdom; the other is that the crew will be persuaded by Donkin to accept his attitude, his ignorance. Although neither of the probabilities is ever absent, one or the other is always dominant. It is here that Conrad's selection is apparent, and it is here that his chapter divisions take on significance. For Conrad has selected, arranged, and represented his events so that the dominant probability shifts from chapter to chapter; but, in addition to this alternation there is also an ascending order of intensity of the probabilities until the climax in the one is reached when the crew is brought to almost open rebellion by Donkin and the climax in the other is reached when the sight of land brings Jimmy's death (proving Singleton infallible in his primitive logic) and the crew, through the voice of Belfast, shouts its new-found wisdom to the reluctant dead: "Jimmy, be a man!"

The central incident of the first chapter is the mustering of the crew, which enables Conrad to introduce to us in a some-what systematic way the real protagonist of his story, the crew (just as, at the end of the novel, the device of the paying-off enables him to bring the individual members of the crew before the reader's eye once more for a last glimpse). Both lines of probability are established. Although the crew spots Donkin for what he is, he knows "how to conquer the naive instincts of that crowd." But it is Singleton as symbol that dominates the chapter, which, significantly, ends with the long description of his now forgotten shipmates of the past, the "everlasting children of the mysterious sea."

In Chapter Two, however, the dominant symbol shifts. The crew, in its doubts and uneasiness about the newly-discovered omnipresent companion of James Wait, goes to old Singleton for advice. The oracle hands down his deci-sion, "Why, of course he will die," and the crew has some-thing definite to which to cling—but only for a moment, for Donkin is quick to twist and make meaningless the oracle's words, and the crew, easily persuaded, begins to hate Singleton. Wisdom is pitted against ignorance, and igno-rance, for the moment, is triumphant. Donkin's attitude toward Wait (or death) prevails, and its disruption of the peaceful life of the ship is detailed in the final lines of the chapter: "He [Wait] overshadowed the ship. Invulnerable in his promise of speedy corruption he trampled on our self-respect, he demonstrated to us daily our want of moral courage: he tainted our lives."

But, as the crew had at first reckoned without Donkin, so Donkin had reckoned without the sea. Donkin's triumph is short-lived, for again, in Chapter Three, symbol is pitted against symbol, and wisdom comes off best. In the struggle to survive the furious storm, in the struggle to free James Wait from his death-trap, in the struggle to right the ship, Donkin is conspicuously absent, Singleton quietly but courageously fulfilling his duty. It is natural that there would follow from the crew contempt for the cowardly Donkin and respect for the steadfast Singleton. An image which seems to sum up the whole of Singleton's wisdom closes yet dominates our memory of the entire chapter: "He steered with care."

The "perfect wisdom," however, which the sea has so generously conferred and which Singleton has so admirably demonstrated, is not easily remembered. In Chapter Four, Donkin skulks about, sowing the seeds of dissension: "We abominated the creature and could not deny the luminous truth of his contentions." When the Captain, attempting to play along with the Nigger's great pretence, orders Wait to remain in his cabin, Donkin seizes the opportunity, his last great chance, to stir the men to the point of open revolt. In the confusion that follows Donkin's throwing of the belaying pin, in the midst of the muttering and rebellious men, Singleton stands "monumental, indistinct." It is at this climactic point that the two symbols at war with each other come face to face: "Singleton peered downwards with puzzled attention, as though he couldn't find him.—'Damn you!' he said, vaguely, giving it up." "Unspeakable" wisdom cannot communicate with unfathomable ignorance. It is with an ambiguous silence that, the next morning, the crew watches the Captain dress down Donkin; but Donkin's influence has already passed its greatest height.

It is not, however, until, in the last chapter, after Jimmy's death, that the crew sees the folly of its false attitude toward the Nigger alive and, confronted by the proof of his prophecies come true, penetrates to the primitive wisdom of old Singleton. The courage it could not give Jimmy alive it attempts to instil in him in death. Only Donkin is absent at

Jimmy's funeral. He has not only been "judged and cast out by the august silence of [the immortal sea's] might," but, after the ship has reached port, and the men are being paid off for the voyage, when he invites his shipmates for a drink (to be paid for with Jimmy's money), "no one moved. There was a silence; a silence of blank faces and stony looks." The rejection of Donkin's ignorance is finally complete, and Singleton's primitive wisdom is at last triumphant. The crew has passed from diversity based on ignorance through a false unity based on the lie perpetrated by Donkin, to, finally, the true "knot" of solidarity based on genuine insight into the meaning of life and death. It has become the kind of crew that Singleton had known in his youth.

THE RICH, METAPHORICAL STYLE

The style of *Nigger* has received a kind of praise that is in reality damning to the work as a whole; it has been assumed that the cadence and the implicit meanings of the highly metaphorical language have some value which bear very little or no relation to the "story" or to the center of the novel. Almost any page offers abundant examples of the richness of Conrad's style:

> At night, through the impenetrable darkness of earth and heaven, broad sheets of flame waved noiselessly; and for half a second the becalmed craft stood out with its mast and rigging, with every sail and every rope distinct and black in the centre of a fiery outburst, like a charred ship enclosed in a globe of fire. And, again, for long hours she remained lost in a vast universe of night and silence where gentle sighs wandering here and there like forlorn souls, made the still sails flutter as in sudden fear, and the ripple of a beshrouded ocean whisper its compassion afar—in a voice mournful, immense, and faint . . .

The imagery here, as throughout the book, is not decorative but functional: at the very heart of the novel is the search for meaning, the search for wisdom; the words seem to explore the scene, the sea, the universe in search of that meaning and wisdom. And if the crew is supposed to achieve wisdom in its voyage on the *Narcissus,* is not the reader also meant to receive a "glimpse of truth" in his voyage with Conrad? The "magic suggestiveness" of the style is not mere superficial trimming: it probes beneath the surfaces for those insights which are to bring the crew (and perhaps the reader) the primitive, the fundamental wisdom of life and death.

The Ambiguous Beginning of "Heart of Darkness"

Richard Adams

Richard Adams analyzes the title and opening paragraphs of "Heart of Darkness," showing that neither
gives the reader clues regarding the subject matter
and focus of the story. Adams offers possible meanings of the title and possible interpretations of the setting and the group of five men setting out on a journey. Adams suggests that the reader is prepared to
eavesdrop on the story "Heart of Darkness." Richard
Adams is professor of English at California State
University in Sacramento. He has written school
texts—*Appropriate English* and *Teaching
Shakespeare*—and published editions of works by
Shakespeare, Conrad, Schaffer, and Iris Murdoch.

Many works of fiction, particularly those written before the
end of the nineteenth century, provide us with some notion of
their subject-matter or focus before we actually embark on a
reading of the text. They do so by means of their title-pages.
One, for instance, purports to be an account of the travels of a
man named Gulliver, while another proclaims itself to be the
autobiographical narrative of a clergyman from the town of
Wakefield. With a third, we are led to expect a study of the
kind of provincial life carried on in a place called
Middlemarch. Other titles reveal in advance the identity of a
pivotal character or characters—from Pamela and Joseph
Andrews and Jane Eyre to Emma and Dombey (and his son)
and Tess and Jude. The names themselves may not tell us
much about what to expect in terms either of personality or of
career, but at least they give us some idea of whom we should
be watching. Similarly, with *North and South* or *The Mill on
the Floss* or *A Tale of Two Cities* we are prepared for some

kind of geographical focus, whether fictitious or real. Still other titles—such as Jane Austen's *Persuasion, Pride and Prejudice* and *Sense and Sensibility*—indicate key ideas or themes or ruling passions.

With *Heart of Darkness,* first published in the spring of 1899, the case is rather different. The phrase is ambiguous, deeply suggestive and logically problematical. At first sight, it is difficult to envisage what kind of signpost to the text it can possibly be.

The ambiguity derives from our natural uncertainty over the force of the word 'of': does it signify composition or location? Are we about to learn about a heart made of darkness— a heart that *is* somehow dark—or a place which lies at the very centre of an area of darkness? That Conrad intended this ambiguity is suggested by the fact that, though he consistently referred to the piece during its composition as *The Heart of Darkness,* a title which tends to favour the 'location' signification, he dropped the definite article on publication.

THE VARIOUS MEANINGS OF 'HEART' AND 'DARKNESS'

Then there is the matter of the range of commonly accepted meanings and associations of 'heart' and 'darkness', and the fact that the two words stand, in many respects, at opposite poles. 'Heart' has a powerful positive force: from its primary denotation of the physical organ on which all animal life depends, it comes to be representative of the life-force itself, as well as of life-enhancing qualities and emotions such as goodness, compassion, courage, love. 'Darkness', on the other hand, has distinctly negative overtones. In a whole host of world mythologies, it is associated with chaos and disorder, the condition to combat which light and life were created. The term 'the Dark Ages' was coined to identify a period of relative unenlightenment in the cultural and intellectual life of early medieval Europe. Because human beings do not naturally function well in the dark, it came to be thought of as the home and haven of all those things—intangible as well as tangible—of which people were unsure or fearful or suspicious. It suggested the unknown, the unknowable, the unintelligible, the ignorant, the sinister, the secret. The English language still abounds in expressions which reflect these associations: a friend asks me what I have been doing lately and, in telling him, I extract a promise that he will 'keep it dark'. In ensuring that other members of our circle are kept ignorant of my activities in this way, I am deliberately leaving them 'in the dark'. But because these other people are aware that I am up to something, without knowing exactly what that something is, they begin to think of me as a 'dark horse' and to speak of my activities—perhaps ironically, perhaps not—as 'dark deeds'.

From such negative attributions, it is but a short step to the fundamental association of darkness with evil. For pre-electric man, darkness was the impenetrable cloak under which crimes and diabolical acts of all kinds were committed: not for nothing was Satan known as 'the Prince of Darkness'. In medieval and Renaissance art, he was indeed commonly portrayed as being black-faced, as were the hapless souls that fell into his grasp. Shakespeare's Macbeth greets the servant who brings him news of the arrival of the English force that is to topple him from power with the curse 'the devil damn thee black'.

It was a perverse and unhealthy logic that extended these associations of ignorance and evil to the negro—the 'darky', as he was called in popular slang—the aboriginal inhabitant of Africa, the 'dark' continent. The conversion of pagan tribes to Christianity and their political and social 'improvement' were figuratively expressed as the bringing of light into a dark wilderness, the benign imposition on chaos of a productive order.

THE COMPLEXITY OF TWO YOKED METAPHORS

The title *Heart of Darkness* is, then, crammed with complex and shifting associations. For Ian Watt,[1] it consists of more than the mere yoking together of two stock metaphors as a means of designating, on the one hand, the centre of benighted Africa, and on the other, a quintessentially evil person (one whose heart is literally made of darkness). He draws attention to the logical implausibility of attributing to the more concrete of the two terms, 'heart', a strategic centrality within a formless and infinite abstraction. 'How', he asks, 'can something inorganic like darkness have an organic centre of life and feeling? How can a shapeless absence of light compact itself into a shaped and pulsing presence?' The problem Watt identifies here is compounded, moreover, by the moral paradox of a 'good' entity (the heart) exercising

1. in *Conrad in the Nineteenth Century.* Los Angeles: University of California Press, 1979.

control over an 'evil' one (darkness).

As we turn to the text for the first time, we need to be aware that the title *Heart of Darkness* does not work at all in the way that *Nicholas Nickleby* and *Crotchet Castle* or— among Conrad's own writings—*Typhoon* and *The Nigger of the Narcissus* work. If we deduce from it anything about the narrative we are about to encounter, perhaps it should be that that narrative may also have its ambiguities, its suggestiveness and its problems of logic.

Any reader of Conrad who comes to *Heart of Darkness* reared exclusively on a diet of the author's sea-stories might be excused, after glancing at the opening paragraphs, for thinking that he or she was about to be served up with more of the same. The *Nellie,* for all that she is temporarily becalmed on the Thames near Gravesend, is bound downriver towards the sea, where any number of adventures may be awaiting her. And, as if to reinforce the impression that this is indeed to be a tale of the sea and ships, the text is liberally seasoned with the sort of technical jargon likely to pack the average reader smartly off to a glossary of nautical terms for assistance. We are told that 'the *Nellie,* a cruising yawl, swung to her anchor' and that 'the flood had made' so that 'the only thing for it was to come to'. There is mention of 'the offing', of 'peaked' sails and 'varnished sprits'.

With the third paragraph, however, there comes a shift of emphasis. We learn that, for all his nautical and reassuringly pilot-like appearance, the boat's captain is not a professional sailor but a company director. Or rather, the other way about: 'The Director of Companies was our captain and our host.' The picture begins to focus more clearly: the narrator's companions are weekend sailors, men engaged in city business of one kind or another, invited by the *Nellie*'s owner to join him for a social cruise down the Thames.

THE GROUP OF FIVE MEN

The entire group consists of five men, identified for us as the Director, the Lawyer, the Accountant, Marlow (the only one of them referred to by name and the only one, as we are later told, who is still a professional seaman) and the narrator. The bond between them is the fact that they have all at some time in their lives 'followed the sea'. The narrator refers to this fact at the beginning of the fourth paragraph, where he also touches, in passing, on his having said as much 'somewhere'

else. This somewhere is at the beginning of Conrad's narrative 'Youth', where the identical company is to be found 'sitting around a mahogany table that reflected the bottle, the
claret-glasses, and our faces as we leaned on our elbows' and
it is made clear that all five of its members had started life in
the merchant service. None of the men is described in any
great detail in the opening pages of *Heart of Darkness;* however, in referring briefly to the appearance or actions of each,
the narrator flashes across the reader's consciousness a number of ideas and images that are developed later in the story.

With the first mention of the Director, for instance, we are
reminded of the deceptiveness of appearances. As he stands
in the bow of his boat and gazes seaward he arouses in his
companions feelings of affection and deep trust. The narrator remarks that he looks like a pilot, 'which to a seaman is
trustworthiness personified', and suggests that he ought to
be working 'out there in the luminous estuary'. But he is not:
his employment lies behind him, in the city of London,
'within the brooding gloom'. The suggestion is that any kind
of appearance, whether good or bad, is not to be taken on
face value.

The Lawyer and Accountant are treated to rather briefer
descriptions. The former, who seems to be the senior member of the party, is stretched out on the deck, enjoying the
benefit—on account 'of his many years and many virtues'—
of the only cushion and the only rug available. The latter has
brought out a box of dominoes and is halfheartedly building
little structures ('toying architecturally') with the pieces.
The narrator's use of the word 'bones' reminds us that, prior
to mass-production, dominoes were often made of ebony
inlaid with bone or ivory, and that bone and ivory were for
centuries mistakenly believed to be the same substance.

Last to be mentioned is Marlow, whose sitting position is
described by the narrator with great precision:

> Marlow sat cross-legged right aft, leaning against the
> mizzen-mast. He had sunken cheeks, a yellow complexion, a
> straight back, an ascetic aspect, and, with his arms dropped,
> the palms of hands outwards, resembled an idol.

As William Bysshe Stein has pointed out, Marlow is here sitting in the so-called lotus posture, familiar to us from its representation in the Buddhist art of India and the Orient.[2] This

---

2. in "The Lotus Posture and the *Heart of Darkness*," *Modern Fiction Studies*, II, 2
(Summer 1957), pp. 167–70.

posture is the one adopted as a prerequisite to Yoga meditation, contemplation and absorption, and it suggests that Marlow 'is ready to engage in an exercise of intense introspection', with the expectation that it will lead to some kind of personal enlightenment. That we are intended to register this connection is made clear by the fact that the narrator goes on to refer to Marlow's Buddha-like bearing on three further occasions in the course of *Heart of Darkness*.

IMAGES SUGGEST THEMES TO BE DEVELOPED

The untrustworthiness of appearances . . . the idea that people and things may not always be what they seem; a man lying full-length on the deck of a boat; another halfheartedly building little structures with domino pieces . . . bone and ivory . . . something white inlaid, grafted, imposed on something black; a third man composing himself for meditation, self-examination, in the hope of enlightenment: such are the ideas and images that we glimpse at the opening of *Heart of Darkness*, ideas and images whose significance becomes clearer as the story progresses.

The narrator adds nothing about himself to this thumbnail gallery of the *Nellie*'s passengers. However, his observations in the opening pages of the story—for all that he implies that a number of them reflect the corporate consciousness of the group—reveal a sensitive and essentially optimistic being. It is he, for example, who articulates the importance of the sea-bond to him and his companions: 'Besides holding our hearts together through long periods of separation, it had the effect of making us tolerant of each other's yarns—and even convictions.' Their estrangement from the sea has introduced diversity of interest, opinion and attitude among the members of the group. The beliefs that any one of them holds and expresses will not necessarily find sympathy or understanding on the part of the others, though the comradeship born of their shared past experiences ought to be enough to ensure a respectful hearing. Each reserves the right to put his personal construction on the tale that another tells; each makes his own decision about accepting or rejecting the philosophical base on which that tale is reared.

As readers, as eavesdroppers on the narrative of *Heart of Darkness*, we are invited to do the same.

Marlow's Role in "Heart of Darkness"

Daniel R. Schwarz

Many scholars maintain that Marlow's voyage upriver to a place of evil symbolizes Conrad's own search for his inner self. Daniel R. Schwarz analyzes the author's and his character's exploration in "Heart of Darkness" in three phases. Marlow begins the Congo journey with traditional Victorian values and beliefs, which the early river experiences challenge. Schwarz argues that Marlow's encounter with Kurtz in the heart of the jungle then presents Marlow's confrontation with his own inner darkness and his near escape from the lure of the wilderness. Finally, when Marlow lies to Kurtz's intended about her beloved's death, Schwarz maintains that despite Marlow's cynicism and disillusionment, civilized people must act as if goodness and faith will prevail. Daniel R. Schwarz has taught at Cornell University in New York. He is the author of several books of criticism, including *Conrad: The Later Fiction* and *Reading Joyce's "Ulysses,"* and a contributor to journals and several collections of critical essays.

Let us consider why Conrad created Marlow. As Conrad's 1894–1900 letters reveal, for him fiction writing is a self-conscious process in which he tests and explores his intellectual and moral identity. Except for brief moments of despair, Conrad believed in the essential value of self-knowledge and self-exploration. He created Marlow to explore himself. . . .

The subject of 'Heart of Darkness' is primarily Marlow, but the presence of Conrad is deeply engraved on every scene. Marlow's effort to come to terms with the Congo experience, especially Kurtz, is the crucial activity that engaged Conrad's imagination. Marlow's consciousness is the arena of the tale. . . .

Excerpted from Daniel R. Schwarz, *Conrad:* Almayer's Folly *to* Under Western Eyes (Ithaca, NY: Cornell University Press, 1980). Copyright © 1980 by Daniel R. Schwarz. Reprinted by permission of Macmillan UK.

MARLOW'S MORAL VIEWS

Marlow begins as if he were recollecting a spiritual voyage of self-discovery: 'It seemed somehow to throw a kind of light on everything about me—and into my thoughts. It was sombre enough too—and pitiful—not extraordinary in any way—not very clear either. No, not very clear. And yet it seemed to throw a kind of light'. As Marlow engages in an introspective monologue, the catalyst for which is his recognition that the Thames, too, contained the same potential darkness for the Romans as the Congo does for him, he recalls how he had discovered the pretensions of European civilisations. At first, his morality and point of view are one dimensional. He relies on conventional Victorian conceptions of honour, integrity, discipline, and the intrinsic value of hard work, and glibly indicts those who fail to live up to these abstract conceptions. . . .

Marlow's journey from Europe to the Congo helped prepare him to sympathise with Kurtz. From the outset he was offended by the standards and perspectives of the European imperialists, and gradually, he began to sympathise with the natives against the predatory colonialists. As an idle passenger on a boat taking him to the Congo, he caught glimpses of the inanity which he later encountered as an involved participant. Even then, he saw the fatuity of the 'civilised' French man-of-war's shelling the bush: 'Pop, would go one of the six-inch guns; a small flame would dart and vanish, a little white smoke would disappear, a tiny projectile would give a feeble screech—and nothing happened'.

Soon, more than his Calvinistic belief in the redemptive powers of purposeful labour was offended. He viewed the company's outer station from an ironic standpoint, noticing the neglected machinery, lying like an animal 'carcass'; the 'objectless blasting'; and the native workers, their rags resembling tails, chained together as if they were a team of mules. He mocked the folly of those who put out fires with buckets that have holes in the bottom and who considered diseased and starving men 'enemies' and 'criminals'. His original epistemological stance,[1] dependent not upon a naive idealised conception of the trading company's commercial ventures, but simply upon his belief that European civilisation represents a tradition of humane values, was shaken.

1. the foundation of his beliefs; his basic assumptions

He began to realise that this version of civilisation is not an 'emissary of light', but an instance of exploitative imperialism at its worst. After arriving at the Central Station, Marlow's quest soon focused on discovering an alternative to the amoral pragmatism and cynicism illustrated by the manager and his uncle. The manager's only objection to Kurtz's abominations is that the results were unsatisfactory: 'The district is closed to us for a time. Deplorable! Upon the whole, the trade will suffer'.

MARLOW GAINS SYMPATHY FOR KURTZ

The manager's cynical materialism impelled Marlow to turn to Kurtz. Speaking of the origins of Marlow's commitment to Kurtz, Albert Guerard[2] remarks:

> Marlow commits himself to the yet unseen agent partly because Kurtz 'had come out equipped with moral ideas of some sort.' Anything would seem preferable to the demoralized greed and total cynicism of the others, 'the flabby devil' of the Central Station.

Gradually, as the people he despised maligned Kurtz, he became interested in meeting him. Thus, contrary to his own sense of integrity and dislike of lying or dissembling, he allowed the 'brickmaker', who really was a spy, to believe that he did have influence in Europe. Marlow, desperate to retain his illusions, wanted to meet a man reputed to be an 'emissary of pity, and science, and progress'. The next he heard of Kurtz was in the dialogue between the manager and his uncle when he learned that Kurtz had come three hundred miles up the river only to turn back. When he imagined Kurtz 'setting his face towards the depths of the wilderness', Marlow tried to put the best possible interpretation on his motives: 'Perhaps he was simply a fine fellow who stuck to his work for its own sake'.

The more he became disillusioned, the more Kurtz became the goal of his quest: 'The approach to this Kurtz grubbing for ivory in the wretched bush was beset by as many dangers as though he had been an enchanted princess sleeping in a fabulous castle'. Conrad describes the quest in romance terms to suggest ironically Marlow's kinship with folk and legendary heroes who also search for miracles and magicians to solve their problems and relieve their anxieties. Standing in the blood of his helmsman, Marlow could

2. in *Conrad the Novelist*

only think that Kurtz was dead and would never talk to him. It was as if he were frustrated in a journey to consult an oracle. After discovering that Kurtz had 'taken a high seat among the devils of the land', he did not renounce his existential commitment to Kurtz as 'the nightmare of my choice'; Kurtz still seemed preferable to the hypocrisy and malignity of the Europeans who have deprived language of its meaning, civilisation of its ideals, and life of its purpose. Marlow, formerly a representative of European civilisation, desperately identified with a man he knew to be ostracised by that civilisation. Ironically, Marlow turned only to a different form of greed and egotism; Kurtz's atavistic[3] impulses have a magnitude and purity that contrast with the pettiness and niggling greed of the imperialists.

We do not know how perceptive Marlow was when he met Kurtz, but Marlow *now* knows that Kurtz was without the restraint that even the helmsman and other cannibals had: 'Mr. Kurtz lacked restraint in the gratification of his various lusts . . .[;] there was something wanting in him—some small matter which, when the pressing need arose, could not be found under his magnificent eloquence.' . . .

Originally, Kurtz had 'set up and [bowed] down before' a benevolent idea, but when the wilderness had 'sealed his soul to its own by the inconceivable ceremonies of some devilish initiation', Kurtz's idea became its own solipsistic[4] parody: 'My intended, my ivory, my station, my river, my—'.

PREOCCUPATION WITH WORK DIVERTS ATTENTION FROM THE DARKNESS

For Marlow piloting the steamer is an important psychic buffer with which to keep the inner darkness at bay: 'When you have to attend . . . to the mere incidents of the surface, the reality—the reality, I tell you—fades. The inner truth is hidden—luckily, luckily. But I felt it all the same; I felt often its mysterious stillness watching me at my monkey tricks, just as it watches you fellows performing on your respective tightropes . . .' . But the man aware of his place in an indifferent cosmos must commit himself to some ideals beyond himself.

> The earth for us is a place to live in, where we must put up with sights, with sounds, with smells, too, by Jove!—breathe

3. traits or behavior reverting to the primitive   4. the theory that the self is the only thing that can be known, that it is the only reality

dead hippo, so to speak and not be contaminated. And there, don't you see? your strength comes in, the faith in your ability for the digging of unostentatious holes to bury the stuff in— your power of devotion, not to yourself, but to an obscure, back-breathing business.

The commitments of innumerable individuals to their respective responsibilities make it possible for mankind to cope collectively with the indifferent objective world. While the surrender of self to function has its dehumanising aspects, civilisation depends on the countless souls who seem to exist for and be defined by their tasks. The helmsman illustrates the beneficial effects of work: 'He ought to have been clapping his hands and stamping his feet on the bank, instead of which he was hard at work, a thrall to strange witchcraft, full of improving knowledge'. Marlow gradually learned that once he leaves the surface, there is no epistemological map for the 'inner truth'. Well before he met Kurtz, he discovered that conventional standards had not prepared him for understanding man's complex antecedents and potential for evil. While Marlow could deal with the manager, the persistent presence of the wilderness over-whelmed him with its 'lurking death', 'hidden evil' and 'pro-found darkness of its heart'. . . .

For a brief time he had, or *believed he had*, discovered a 'rent' in the veil of the 'impenetrable darkness' of Kurtz's soul, and had gone 'through the ordeal of looking into [Kurtz's soul] myself'. However, the real reason for his commitment is that Kurtz has been the catalyst for Marlow's looking into his own soul and learning fundamental things about himself and mankind.

KURTZ SYMBOLIZES MARLOW'S INNER STRUGGLE

Marlow invests Kurtz with values which fulfil his own need to embody his threat of the jungle in one tangible creature. If Kurtz is considered the centre of the 'heart of darkness', the business of following Kurtz and winning the 'struggle' enables Marlow to believe that he had conquered a symbol of the atavistic, debilitating effects of the jungle. This belief is central to his interpretation of the journey's significance. For Marlow, capturing Kurtz after he escapes symbolises a personal victory over darkness. Increasingly, he had been attracted to the jungle by the urge to go ashore for 'a howl and a dance'. Having given in to his primitive urges, Kurtz appropriately crawls away on all fours. Marlow recalls how he, too, was tempted by savage impulses and confused his heartbeat with the beat of the natives' drums. Uncharacteristically, he thought of giving Kurtz a 'drubbing'. He was 'strangely cocksure of himself' and enjoyed stalking his prey. His assertion that 'he left the track' indicates that he, too, is in danger now that he is alone in the jungle; he thinks that he might never get back. But when Marlow confronts Kurtz, he recalls, 'I seemed to come to my senses, I saw the danger in its right proportion'. To him, the confrontation represents coming to terms with the dark potential within himself against the background of primitive and unspeakable rites. But he does not surrender to the appeal of the wilderness precisely because he has internalised the restraints imposed by civilisation.

That Kurtz has achieved a 'moral victory' may very well be a necessary illusion for Marlow. But did Kurtz pronounce a verdict on his reversion to primitivism and achieve the 'supreme moment of complete knowledge'? Or is this what Marlow desperately wants to believe? Coming from a man who 'could get himself to believe anything', how credible is Marlow's interpretation that 'The horror! The horror!' is 'an affirmation, a moral victory paid for by innumerable defeats, by abominable terrors, by abominable satisfactions'? When Kurtz had enigmatically muttered, 'Live rightly, die, die. . .', Marlow had wondered 'Was he rehearsing some speech in his sleep, or was it a fragment of a phrase from some newspaper article?' Marlow had just remarked that Kurtz's voice 'survived his strength to hide in the magnificent folds of eloquence the barren darkness of his heart'. If Kurtz had kicked himself loose of the earth, how can Kurtz pronounce a verdict on his ignominious return to civilisation or an exclamation elicited from a vision of his own imminent death? For the reader, Kurtz remains a symbol of how the human ego can expand infinitely to the point where it tries to will its own apotheosis.[5]

MARLOW LIES TO KURTZ'S INTENDED

The lie to the Intended is another crucial moment of self-definition. Marlow's return to his homeland as something of a misanthrope suggests Gulliver's return from the land of

5. divine rank or stature; deification

MARLOW'S ROLE IN "HEART OF DARKNESS"

In the closing paragraphs of "Heart of Darkness," Marlow conceals the truth about Kurtz's end to save Kurtz's Intended from the heartbreaking reality.

"'His end,' said I, with dull anger stirring in me, 'was in every way worthy of his life.'

"'And I was not with him,' she murmured. My anger subsided before a feeling of infinite pity.

"'Everything that could be done—' I mumbled.

"'Ah, but I believed in him more than any one on earth—more than his own mother, more than—himself. He needed me! Me! I would have treasured every sigh, every word, every sign, every glance.'

"I felt like a chill grip on my chest. 'Don't,' I said, in a muffled voice.

"'Forgive me. I–I–have mourned so long in silence—in silence. . . . You were with him—to the last? I think of his loneliness. Nobody near to understand him as I would have understood. Perhaps no one to hear. . . .'

"'To the very end,' I said, shakily. 'I heard his very last words. . . .' I stopped in a fright.

the Houyhnhnms. Disappointed and resentful, he actually detested the people of the 'sepulchral city' scurrying about

> . . . to dream their insignificant and silly dreams. They trespassed upon my thoughts. They were intruders whose knowledge of life was to me an irritating pretence, because I felt so sure they could not possibly know the things I knew.

But he brought himself to participate in the 'silly dreams' in order to protect the Intended's sensibilities. Knowing that the lie hurts no one, he allows the Intended to believe in Kurtz. Marlow consciously adjusted his morality to suit the needs of others, and he deliberately took part in a scene which required not only absolute self-control, but the use of the disingenuous tactics he despised. The ability to function morally within the complexities of 'civilized' life was the final test of his personal development. [Critic] Walter F. Wright puts it well: 'If he had told the girls the simple facts, he would have acknowledged that the pilgrims in their cynicism had the truth, that goodness and faith were the unrealities.' Marlow's lie to the Intended, allowing her to sustain her faith, is paradoxically a rejection of indifference and

"'Repeat them,' she murmured in a heartbroken tone. 'I want—I want—something—something—to—to live with.'

"I was on the point of crying at her, 'Don't you hear them?' The dusk was repeating them in a persistent whisper all around us, in a whisper that seemed to swell menacingly like the first whisper of a rising wind. 'The horror! the horror!'

"'His last word—to live with,' she insisted. 'Don't you understand I loved him—I loved him—I loved him!'

"I pulled myself together and spoke slowly.

"'The last word he pronounced was—your name.'

"I heard a light sigh and then my heart stood still, stopped dead short by an exulting and terrible cry, by the cry of inconceivable triumph and of unspeakable pain. 'I knew it—I was sure!' . . . She knew. She was sure. I heard her weeping; she had hidden her face in her hands. It seemed to me that the house would collapse before I could escape, that the heavens would fall upon my head. But nothing happened. The heavens do not fall for such a trifle. Would they have fallen, I wonder, if I had rendered Kurtz that justice which was his due? Hadn't he said he wanted only justice? But I couldn't. I could not tell her. It would have been too dark—too dark altogether. . . ."

Joseph Conrad, "Heart of Darkness," 1899.

cynicism; as he acknowledges, to tell the truth 'would have been too dark—too dark altogether'. Marlow has journeyed back from the inner reality to the surface world where illusions are essential. He recognised the place in a civilised community of both relative morality and humane responses to the needs of others. . . .

MARLOW DISCOVERS NO INNER TRUTH

Marlow returns from his journey with no inner truth, no symbolic light to clarify the darkness. The equation of the Roman voyage up the Thames and Marlow's up the Congo suggests an important parallel. That Marlow says 'this also has been'—not 'this also was'—'one of the dark places on the earth' denies the idea of humanity's progressive evolution, still a widely held view in the 1890s, by showing that the manifestation of barbaric impulses is a continuous possibility. The essential nature of Europeans and natives is the same: 'The mind is capable of anything—because everything is in it, all the past as well as all the future'. Conrad stresses that illusions are not only a defence against reversion to primitive life, but the basis of civilisation. . . .

That self-fulfilment and a limited self-knowledge are ultimate goals in a world in which there is a disjunction between subjective and objective is acknowledged by Marlow: 'Droll thing life is—that mysterious arrangement of merciless logic for a futile purpose. The most you can hope from it is some knowledge of yourself—that comes too late—a crop of unextinguishable regrets'. In this *Zeitgeist*,[6] man cannot discover absolute values; discovering 'principles' won't do; what he searches for is a sustaining illusion, a 'deliberate belief'. In a famous letter to [his friend and critic Edward] Garnett, written a few months after Conrad finished 'Heart of Darkness', Conrad complained:

> I am like a man who has lost his gods. My efforts seem unrelated to anything in heaven and everything under heaven is impalpable to the touch like shapes of mist.
>
> Even writing to a friend . . . does not give me a sense of reality. All is illusion—the words written, the mind at which they are aimed, the truth they are intended to express, the hands that will hold the paper, the eyes that will glance at the lines. Every image floats vaguely in a sea of doubt—and the doubt itself is lost in an unexplored universe of incertitudes.

Marlow echoes Conrad's despair with the ability of language to communicate his subjective world: 'Do you see him? Do you see the story? Do you see anything? It seems to me I am trying to tell you a dream—making a vain attempt, because no relation of a dream can convey the dream-sensation, that commingling of absurdity, surprise and bewilderment in a tremor of struggling revolt, that notion of being captured by the incredible which is of the very essence of dreams. . .' . Marlow concludes this passage by generalising his solitude: 'We live, as we dream—alone.' The meanings of words like 'civilized', 'workers', 'criminals', 'enemies', and 'rebels' have been blurred as if the gift of language itself had been corrupted by civilisation.

THE SUCCESSFUL EFFECTS OF LANGUAGE

Yet paradoxically Kurtz's effect on Marlow illustrates the power of language. Kurtz is at first presented as a master of language. The hypnotic effect of Kurtz's voice has a kinship with the incantations of the savages rather than the syntac-

6. the spirit of the time; the outlook characteristic of a period or generation

tical patterns of ordinary discourse. Eloquence is Kurtz's gift, and his report is 'a beautiful piece of writing' whose peroration makes Marlow 'tingle with enthusiasm': 'This was the unbounded power of eloquence—of words—of burning noble words'. Anticipating Jim on Patusan, Kurtz's fiction becomes his life; but unlike Jim who models the standards of his imaginative world upon the home world, Kurtz's world takes shape from forbidden dreams of being worshipped and from libidinous needs that brook no restraint. In transforming his imaginative world into reality, Kurtz 'had kicked himself loose of the earth. . . . He had kicked the very earth to pieces. He was alone . . .' . For a moment Marlow lived in Kurtz's world, only to have had the 'magic current of phrases' interrupted by the grotesque appendix, 'Exterminate all the brutes!' However pernicious, the appendix does communicate and belies the idea that language is solipsistic, even if Kurtz, the demonic artist, is appropriating language to his own uses. Kurtz's words, Marlow recalls, 'were common everyday words—the familiar, vague sounds exchanged on every waking day of life . . . [but] they had behind them, to my mind, the terrific suggestiveness of words heard in dreams, of phrases spoken in nightmares'. It is from this point that the narrative includes the gestures of the savage mistress and the Intended; the beating of the drums, the shrill cry of the sorrowing savages; and the development of Kurtz into Marlow's own symbol of moral darkness and atavistic reversion. Marlow's recurring nightmare begins not only to compete with his effort to use language discursively and mimetically, but to establish a separate, more powerful telling. This more inclusive tale, not so much told as revealed by Marlow as he strains for the signs and symbols which will make his experience intelligible, transcends his more conventional discourse. Conrad shows that these instinctive and passionate outbursts, taking the form of gestures, chants, and litany, represent a tradition, a core of experience, that civilised man has debased. In a brilliant surrealistic touch, Conrad makes Marlow's consciousness an echo chamber for the haunting sounds of his 'culminating' experience. After recalling that Kurtz 'was little more than a voice', the past rushes in to disrupt the present effort to give shape and meaning to his narrative: 'And I heard him—it—this voice—other voices—all of them were so little more than voices—and the memory of that time itself lingers

around me, impalpable, *like* a dying vibration of one immense jabber, silly, atrocious, sordid, savage, or simply
mean, without any kind of sense. Voices, voices—even the
girl herself—now—' (emphasis mine). The temporary
breakdown of Marlow's syntax in the passage dramatises
the resistance of his experience to ordinary discourse, even
as the simile comparing Kurtz's voice to an 'immense jabber'
reveals the challenge of his nightmare to language.

Yet Marlow's decision to narrate his experience is predi-
cated upon at least a tentative faith that language is the vehicle of order, reason, and symbolic light which would serve
as his intellectual guide to explore the mystery and darkness
of the human soul. Marlow's tale deeply affects the nameless
listener who becomes our narrator: 'I raised my head. The
offing was barred by a black bank of clouds, and the tranquil
waterway leading to the uttermost ends of the earth flowed
sombre under an overcast sky—seemed to lead into the
heart of an immense darkness'. . . .

The adaptation of Marlow's brooding tone and style of
expression indicates that Marlow had communicated something of his experience. That Marlow communicates demon-
strates that man does not live completely alone as he had
claimed, and implies that language can establish the 'fellowship' and 'solidarity' that both Marlow and his creator seek.

Africans in "Heart of Darkness"

Harold R. Collins

Harold R. Collins distinguishes the differences between the coastal Africans, who have lost the moral order of their native society, and the upriver cannibals, who still retain the moral knowledge of their tribe. Collins argues that Marlow understands the detribalized helmsman and compares him to Kurtz; they are both "isolates" who die because they no longer possess the moral restraints their respective societies impose. Harold R. Collins has taught at the University of Connecticut and Kent State University in Ohio. He has contributed to journals on African literature, has edited *Critical Perspectives on Amos Tuluola*, and is the author of *Amos Tuluola: Folk Novelist Among the Ghosts.*

We have to be very chary about pontificating on the "totality of meaning" of "Heart of Darkness." Of course, wherever we look we see wonderful arrangements. Suppose we consider some humble fellows who have not received much attention in critical discussions, those cannibal crewmen and the unstable native helmsman. If we examine the episodes in which they figure and the comments Marlow makes upon their conduct we shall observe that Conrad has involved these apparently insignificant black men in the main theme. To be sure, "Heart of Darkness" is primarily concerned with the moral isolation of a man much more impressive than the hungry cannibals and the flustered native helmsman. . . .

Marlow's first casual mention of the cannibal crewmen associates them with the work motive, a prominent motive intimately connected with the testing of Kurtz. "More than once she (the steamboat) had to wade for a bit, with twenty cannibals splashing around and pushing. . . . Fine fellows— cannibals—in their place. They were men one could work

Excerpted from Harold R. Collins, "Kurtz, the Cannibals, and the Second-Rate Helmsman," *Western Humanities Review*, Autumn 1954, pp. 299–310. Reprinted by permission of the *Western Humanities Review*.

with." This compliment ranges the man-eaters with men whom Marlow can respect, those who do real work. . . .

THE VALUE OF WORK

Marlow has a good deal to say about the value of work and its connection with reality. No influential friend, such as the aristocratic brickmaker might imagine, could have served him better than that "battered, twisted, ruined tinpot steamer." She had given him "a chance to come out a bit." To be sure, he doesn't like work itself; he likes "what is in the work,—the chance to find yourself. Your own reality—for yourself, not for others—what no other man can ever know." When Marlow feels the "mysterious stillness" of the Congo's "inner truth" watching him at his work, his work seems mere "monkey tricks," yet he can "find himself" in those "tricks" because he does them well.

If work discloses this kind of truth to Marlow, it also, mercifully, protects him from another kind. While he worries about the elusive channel, hidden banks, sunken stones, snags, leaky pipes, and the savage fireman, the oppressive "reality" of the Congo jungle, whose stillness suggests "an implacable force brooding over an inscrutable intention," fades in his consciousness. "The inner truth is hidden— luckily, luckily." He has no time for "creepy thoughts" about the primitive men on the shore who "howled and leaped, and spun, and made horrid faces." His work gives him no time to think of his "remote kinship with this wild and passionate uproar."

He certainly does not imply that work means to the cannibals what it means to him, only that the man who does real work is a better man than the one who can not or will not, even though the worker is a black savage. Sham work Marlow calls "unreal." He sees a good deal of such sham work in the Congo: the French war against their native "enemies," the punishment of "criminals," the hiring of "workers" by time contract, the pilgrims' "show of work," Kurtz's execution of "rebels." Incidentally, Conrad is not idealizing Congo cannibals when he has his narrator say that these savages with whom one could work were "fine fellows.". . .

When the tinpot steamer is fog-bound just below Kurtz's Inner Station and the pilgrims are "greatly discomposed" at the prospect of an attack, the cannibal crewmen are calm, have "an alert, naturally interested expression on their faces." Several of them grin as they haul on the anchor chain. Several exchange "short grunting phrases which seemed to settle the matter to their satisfaction." Their headman coolly advises Marlow to catch some of the natives on the shore and give them to the crew, who would "eat 'im." Now observe that these savages do not behave at all like such "reclaimed" Africans as the prisoners' guard with the unmilitary bearing and the rascally grin, the manager's boy, who announces Kurtz's death "with scathing contempt," and the unstable helmsman, who conducts himself so imprudently during the attack from Kurtz's "adorers." The guard, the manager's boy, and the helmsman are what the anthropologists now call "detribalized natives"; that is, natives alienated from the old tribal life. The crewmen are still raw bush savages, the sort of Africans most white travelers and settlers prefer to more civilized Africans. Recruited from a place 800 miles from Kurtz's station at Stanley Falls (somewhere between Bolobo and Kinshassa, the steamer's home port), they have lived a considerable distance from the coast, from which white influences radiated.

Marlow speaks of the "dignified and profoundly pensive attitude" of the headman who makes the cannibalistic proposal. It may seem strange, but uncivilized savages are dignified. The cannibals in "Heart of Darkness" seem to have the dignity and self-assurance of Africans who still have the comfortable feeling of being valued members of some native social order, who have not been in contact with the whites long enough to be troubled by the social disabilities of a civilized social order, shamed by their ignorance of European technical knowledge, confused by the conflicting moral imperatives of two cultures. They are probably sustained— as Kurtz is not—by the warm close ties of an organic society.

Diedrich Westermann's description[1] of the social conditions of the uncivilized African seems pertinent to our discussion of Marlow's cannibals: "The consciousness of being a well protected member of a group gives the individual a definite . . . dignity . . . He knows no crawling, humility, no slavish flattery, and he is not easily embarrassed. Within his own circle he is never in a position when he does not know how to behave or what to do. In a primitive community work is not specialized in the same way as with us and therefore

1. in *The African Today and Tomorrow*, rev. ed. (London, 1939), pp. 156–57. Westermann is Director of the International Institute of African Languages and Cultures.

THE HELMSMAN'S FATAL LACK OF RESTRAINT

In this excerpt from "Heart of Darkness," Conrad describes the helmsman's undisciplined actions leading to his death.

Arrows, by Jove! We were being shot at! I stepped in quickly to close the shutter on the land-side. That fool-helmsman, his hands on the spokes, was lifting his knees high, stamping his feet, champing his mouth, like a reined-in horse. Confound him! And we were staggering within ten feet of the bank. . . . "Steer her straight," I said to the helmsman. He held his head rigid, face forward; but his eyes rolled, he kept on, lifting and setting down his feet gently, his mouth foamed a little. "Keep quiet!" I said in a fury. I might just as well have ordered a tree not to sway in the wind. . . . A fusillade burst out under my feet. The pilgrims had opened with their Winchesters, and were simply squirting lead into that bush. A deuce of a lot of smoke came up and drove slowly forward. . . . I glanced over my shoulder, and the pilot-house was yet full of noise and smoke when I made a dash at the wheel. The fool-nigger had dropped everything, to throw the shutter open and let off that Martini-Henry. He stood before the wide opening, glaring, and I yelled at him to come back, while I straightened the sudden twist out of that steamboat. . . .

Looking past that mad helmsman, who was shaking the empty rifle and yelling at the shore, I saw vague forms of men running bent double, leaping, gliding, distinct, incomplete, evanescent. Something big appeared in the air before the shutter, the rifle went overboard, and the man stepped back swiftly, looked at me over his shoulder in an extraordinary, profound, familiar manner, and fell upon my feet. The side of his head hit the wheel twice, and the end of what appeared a long cane clattered round and knocked over a little camp-stool. It looked as

the non-expert 'layman' who is helpless in everything that goes beyond his special field of activity does not exist. . . . Every individual is aware of being a valued member of his group subject to no one, and it is natural to him to maintain this same self-assurance in dealing with the white man, to whom in many ways he feels himself superior.". . .

THE POWER OF RESTRAINT

Marlow is not "properly horrified" by the headman's cannibalistic suggestion. Recalling that the pilgrims have thrown most of the cannibals' rotten hippo meat overboard and that

though after wrenching that thing from somebody ashore he had lost his balance in the effort. The thin smoke had blown away, we were clear of the snag, and looking ahead I could see that in another hundred yards or so I would be free to sheer off, away from the bank; but my feet felt so very warm and wet that I had to look down. The man had rolled on his back and stared straight up at me; both his hands clutched that cane. It was the shaft of a spear that, either thrown or lunged through the opening, had caught him in the side just below the ribs; the blade had gone in out of sight, after making a frightful gash; my shoes were full; a pool of blood lay very still, gleaming dark-red under the wheel; his eyes shone with an amazing lustre. The fusillade burst out again. He looked at me anxiously, gripping the spear like something precious, with an air of being afraid I would try to take it away from him. I had to make an effort to free my eyes from his gaze and attend to the steering. . . .

I declare it looked as though he would presently put to us some question in an understandable language; but he died without uttering a sound, without moving a limb, without twitching a muscle. Only in the very last moment, as though in response to some sign we could not see, to some whisper we could not hear, he frowned heavily, and that frown gave to his black death-mask an inconceivably sombre, brooding, and menacing expression. The lustre of inquiring glance faded swiftly into vacant glassiness. . . .

To tell you the truth, I was morbidly anxious to change my shoes and socks. "He is dead," murmured the fellow, immensely impressed. "No doubt about it," said I, tugging like mad at the shoe-laces. . . . I flung one shoe overboard. . . . The other shoe went flying unto the devil-god of that river. I thought, By Jove! it's all over.

Joseph Conrad, "Heart of Darkness," 1899.

their wages of brass wire have not been very useful for purchasing provisions in the riverside villages, he knows that the poor fellows must be very hungry. Indeed he wonders "Why in the name of all the gnawing devils of hunger they didn't go for us—they were thirty to five—and have a good tuck-in for once. . . . They were big powerful men, with not much capacity to weigh the consequences . . .". He supposes that "something restraining, one of those human secrets that baffle probability," has come into play. But what could restrain such wild men? "Restraint! What possible restraint?" Here we have another of the important motives of the story. Even the manager, who would be happy to hang the independent traders providing "unfair competition," has his restraint: he wishes to preserve appearances. As we shall see, the helmsman has no restraint, is like Kurtz in that respect. Those symbolical ornaments on Kurtz's fence signify that "Mr. Kurtz lacked restraint in the gratification of his various lusts.". . .

As Conrad himself says in *Personal Record*, "The part of the inexplicable should be allowed for in the appraising the conduct of men in a world where no explanation is final." The kinds of restraints that may be depended upon to keep a man within moral bounds in ordinary circumstances have not motivated these savages who have resisted the "deviltry of lingering starvation." They just happen to have that "inborn strength" that is needed to fight hunger properly. Only such "inborn strength" would have saved Kurtz in his trial. . . .

The cannibals belong to that vengeful jungle, that darkness, that has tried Kurtz and found him wanting. While the bepatched young Russian is telling Marlow about his wonderful conversations with Kurtz ("We talked of everything . . . Everything! . . . Of love, too.") the crewmen are lounging near by, human illustrations of that Congo savagery from which Kurtz's conversational graces have not been able to save him. The headman turns his "heavy and glittering eyes" upon the young man whose mind Kurtz "had enlarged." At that moment Marlow feels very keenly the power of that Congo scene which has been Kurtz's undoing. "I looked around, and I don't know why, but I assure you that never, never before, did this land, this river, this jungle, the very arch of this blazing sky, appear to me so hopeless and so dark, so impenetrable to human thought, so pitiless to human weakness." If Kurtz's native mistress, "savage and superb, wild-eyed and magnificent," symbolizes the fascination of the Congo scene, the cannibals symbolize its pitiless power, and its reality, which exposes Kurtz's "noble sentiments" as sham.

COMPARING THE HELMSMAN AND KURTZ

It is easy to underestimate the importance of the native helmsman in Marlow's journey to "the farthest point of navigation and the culminating point of [his] experience." Does it not seem odd that he should recall this insignificant black fellow's foolish conduct in such detail and make his death scene almost as impressive as that of Kurtz himself? When Marlow says he is not sure that the "remarkable man" was worth the life they lost in getting to him, he realizes that his listeners will "think it passing strange this regret for a savage who was no more account than a grain of sand in a black Sahara." The reasons he gives for this regret constitute a commentary on the shortcomings of Kurtz.

The helmsman "had done something, he had steered." We have the work motive again. Kurtz has not done any real work in the Congo; his methods are "no methods at all." It is questionable if he has ever done any real work. Was he a painter who wrote for the papers or a journalist who painted, or did he have any regular profession at all? Even Kurtz's cousin back in the "sepulchral city" could not tell "what he had been—exactly." A journalist in that city thinks that Kurtz ought to have been a leader of an extreme party, any extreme party, but political activity of that sort would scarcely qualify as proper work as Marlow understands it.

The helmsman has not, like Kurtz, cut himself loose from all human ties. As a "help," an "instrument," he is in a "kind of partnership" with his captain. His very deficiencies that his captain worries about create a "subtle bond" between the two of them. The "intimate profundity" of that look he gives Marlow when he dies is like a "claim of distant kinship." These human ties mean a great deal to the humble African because he is isolated from his own native society. His conduct in his work gives us the clue for understanding this isolation.

The "athletic black belonging to some coast tribe" is not a good helmsman. He is an "unstable kind of fool," steering "with no end of swagger" while his white man is at his side, but "instantly the prey of an abject funk" the moment he is alone. When Kurtz's "adorers" attack the steamer, he prances about, "stamping his feet, champing his mouth, like a reined-in horse." He leaves the wheel to open the shutter on the land side, fire off the Martini-Henry, and yell at the shore—and gets himself speared for his reckless folly.

Explaining his helmsman's fatal imprudence, Marlow anticipates his comments on the degradation of Kurtz. "Poor fool! If he had only let that shutter alone. He had no restraint, no restraint—just like Kurtz—a tree swayed in the wind." The helmsman has been tested, as the cannibals are tested, as Kurtz has been tested. The cannibals, tormented by

MARLOW LOSES HIS HELMSMAN

In this excerpt, Conrad describes Marlow's feeling of loss as he buries his helmsman in the river.

I missed my late helmsman awfully,—I missed him even while his body was still lying in the pilot-house. Perhaps you will think it passing strange this regret for a savage who was no more account than a grain of sand in a black Sahara. Well, don't you see, he had done something, he had steered; for months I had him at my back—a help—an instrument. It was a kind of partnership. He steered for me. . . .

As soon as I had put on a dry pair of slippers, I dragged him out, after first jerking the spear out of his side, which operation I confess I performed with my eyes shut tight. His heels leaped together over the little doorstep; his shoulders were pressed to my breast; I hugged him from behind desperately. Oh! he was heavy, heavy; heavier than any man on earth, I should imagine. Then without more ado I tipped him overboard. The current snatched him as though he had been a wisp of grass, and I saw the body roll over twice before I lost sight of it for ever. . . . I had made up my mind that if my late helmsman was to be eaten, the fishes alone should have him.

Joseph Conrad, "Heart of Darkness," 1899.

hunger, have refrained from eating the pilgrims. Kurtz, in "utter solitude without a policeman" and "utter silence, where no warning voice of a kind neighbor can be heard," has "lacked restraint in the gratification of his various lusts," has taken a "high seat among the devils of the land." The helmsman almost wrecks the tinpot steamer, endangers the lives of the passengers, and throws his life away; when the fixed standards of conduct of his profession require steady steering, he can not resist the temptation to caper as though he were dancing an old-fashioned African war dance and to help the pilgrims squirt lead into the bush; when he should show his mettle, he merely "shows off."

THE EFFECTS OF DETRIBALIZATION

The helmsman is not dignified and dependable like the cannibals, the "raw bush natives." Anyone at all familiar with modern anthropological studies of the process of "detribalization" and more recent fiction dealing with Africa will be struck by the fact that Conrad is representing "detribalized" natives in the characters of the slovenly prisoners' guard, the ill-conditioned manager's boy, and the second-rate helmsman; he is representing Africans who have been deprived of their traditional beliefs and standards of conduct without having assumed, or being able to assume, those of the white men. The manager's boy and the helmsman have come from coast tribes. Africans from the coast would be much more likely to be partially civilized, be "mission boys," in the white settlers' contemptuous phrase, than would those living up-river, for on the coast white men have long had "factories," or trading posts, and the first missions were established there. We may recall Marlow's ironical comments on these partially civilized Africans: "One of the reclaimed" (the guard), "an improved specimen" (the fireman), "an overfed young negro" (the manager's boy), "thought the world of himself" (the helmsman). In "weaning those ignorant millions from their horrid ways," the Belgian emissaries of light have produced, not dark-skinned gentlemen, but vain creatures whose ways are seldom perfectly agreeable. . . .

When we know that Conrad is describing a detribalized native, the helmsman's bravado, his instability, his lack of restraint, are understandable. An African helmsman's work might well become wearisome to him after its novelty—originally its main attraction for him—had worn off. He would probably regret the old African communal work in the fields, the fishing and hunting, the fashioning of tools, weapons, dug-outs, and personal ornaments, for such work was more interesting to him, more leisurely, and more sociable. An African helmsman might well get into "an abject funk" over his steering, even though his captain had "educated" him. The fireman on the steamer, "an improved specimen," only understands that if he does not tend the boiler properly "the evil spirit inside the boiler" will get terribly angry; he is "a thrall to strange witchcraft." If the African felt that there was strange magic in the steering gear, he would be in a bad plight indeed, for his "respected magician" would not be with him to prescribe countermagic for his solace.

The helmsman seems very silly with his swaggering, his prancing about, his inopportune "gun-play" when he should be steering, but an African in his position might be expected to be very proud to have mastered even a small part of the white men's magical powers, might also be expected to kick up his heels occasionally, as a relief from the deadly dull routine of working for the whites, who seem so unaccountably exacting in their demands. And he would miss the exuberant festivities of the old tribal life: the elaborate funerals, the "burial murders," the poison ordeals, the initiation ceremonies with the companions of his age-group, the rituals for the tribal fetish and for the sacred dead, the communal harvesting with beer-drinking and drum music.

TWO ISOLATES LACKING A MORAL SYSTEM

Probably we would be quite safe in classing the second-rate helmsman with those Conradian characters that the critics have called "isolates." He has been deprived of the restraints and consolations of a social order, as Kurtz has been. And like Kurtz he lacks that "inner strength," that saving "definite belief" which may save the man thus deprived. . . .

Conrad's mentioning of the "rascally grin" on the guard's face and of the impudence and insolence of the manager's boy clearly indicates he realized that the "reclaimed" Africans often had more serious shortcomings than vanity and instability. The African novels of Paton, Cary, and Huxley represent the moral disintegration of tribeless Africans. They illustrate Arthur Jarvis' statement on the "breaking of the tribes," in Paton's *Cry, the Beloved Country* (1948): "The old tribal system was, for all its superstition and witchcraft, a moral system. Our natives today produce criminals and prostitutes and drunkards, not because it is their nature to do so, but because their simple system of order and tradition has been destroyed. It was destroyed by the impact of our civilization.". . .

We have noticed that important motives in "Heart of Darkness" connect the white men with the Africans. Conrad knew that the white men who come to Africa professing to bring progress and light to "darkest Africa" have themselves been deprived of the sanctions of their European social orders; they also have been alienated from the old tribal ways. Thrown upon their own inner spiritual resources— like detribalized natives—they may be utterly damned by their greed, their sloth, and their hypocrisy into moral insignificance, as were the pilgrims, or they may be so corrupted by their absolute power over the Africans that some Marlow will need to lay their memory among the "dead cats of civilization."

Apocalypse Now: A Film Version of "Heart of Darkness"

Gene D. Phillips

On the surface, the film *Apocalypse Now* differs greatly from the novella "Heart of Darkness" since the film concerns the Vietnam War in Southeast Asia and the book concerns the ivory trade in the Belgian Congo in Africa. The film is, however, a frank adaptation of the Conrad tale. Gene D. Phillips cites parallels in the structure of the journey, the voice of the narrator, and the characterization of Kurtz. Gene D. Phillips, English professor at Loyola University in Chicago, teaches fiction and film history. He is the author of *Hemingway and Film; Fiction, Film, and Faulkner;* and *Fiction, Film, and F. Scott Fitzgerald.*

In the spring of 1975 the distinguished American director Francis Coppola (*The Godfather*) told an interviewer that his next film would deal with the Vietnam War. As a starting point for his screenplay Coppola noted that he had selected a six-year-old scenario done by writer-director John Milius (*The Wind and the Lion*) in 1969, based on Conrad's "Heart of Darkness." The script had updated the story to the Vietnam War and turned Kurtz from an ivory trader into a Green Beret officer who defects from the American army and sets up his own army across the Cambodian border where he proceeds to conduct his own private war against the Vietcong. . . .

On the surface it seems that Conrad's novella is very different from Coppola's film. For instance, Conrad's story takes place in the Belgian Congo in the 1890s and focuses on Charles Marlow, a British sailor employed by a European trading firm as captain of one of their steamboats. By contrast, Coppola's film is set in Southeast Asia in the 1960s, and

ᵃᵃᵃᵃᵃᵃᵃᵃᵃᵃᵃᵃᵃᵃᵃᵃᵃ

centers on Benjamin Willard, an American army officer. Yet, as film scholar Linda Cahir points out,[1] although the settings and backgrounds of novella and film are quite different, the manner in which the story is narrated in each instance is "splendidly similar." Here is a brief summary of the fundamental parallels between book and film.

For example, "each tale-proper begins with the protagonist's explanation of how he got the appointment which necessitated his excursion up river," Cahir points out. Marlow is dispatched to steam up the Congo in order to find Mr. Kurtz, an ivory trader who disappeared into the interior and never returned. Willard is mandated to journey up the Mekong River in a navy patrol boat to find Col. Kurtz, who has recruited his own renegade army to fight the Vietcong. In addition, while Marlow and Willard each travel up a primeval river to fulfill their respective assignments, each speculates about the character of the man he is seeking, with the help of the information each has pieced together about him. Furthermore, the last stop for both Marlow and Willard, concludes Cahir, "is the soul-altering confrontation with the mysterious Kurtz."

Moreover, one of the elements of Coppola's film which serves to bring it closer to the original story is employing Willard as the narrator of the film, just as Marlow is the narrator of the novella. Hence the screenplay of *Apocalypse Now* remains most faithful to its source in its attempt to depict the action through flashback, with the narrator's comments on the action heard, voice-over, on the soundtrack. Hence Willard is what Avrom Fleishman calls in his book *Narrated Films* an internal (subjective) narrator, because Willard gives his personal reactions to his own experiences as he narrates them over the soundtrack. By contrast, an external (objective) narrator . . . is so called precisely because he simply reports an objective version of the facts of someone else's life. . . .

It is more difficult to imply in a movie, than it is in a work of fiction, that a given account of past events is being presented from the subjective point of view of one of the characters—as when Willard recalls in his voice-over commentary his initial misgivings about carrying out his secret orders to assassinate Kurtz when he finds him. This is

1. in "Narratological Parallels in Joseph Conrad's 'Heart of Darkness' and Francis Ford Coppola's *Apocalypse Now*," *Literature/Film Quarterly* 20, no. 3 (1992), 182–83

because a film audience is always conscious that it is watching what is being dramatized in flashback on the screen—*not* through the eyes of the character who is narrating the events in question—but through the eyes of the camera. The screenplay may try to retain the subjective dimension of these memories by having the voice of the character who is recalling the event in question surface on the soundtrack occasionally to give his subjective reflections on the flashback as it unfolds on the screen, as is the case in the present film. But the viewer still does not have the sense that he is seeing the flashback from the point of view of the character who is retelling the event. By the same token, while the filmgoer is watching *Lord Jim*, he often forgets that he is supposedly seeing Jim's story through the eyes of Marlow, who narrates that film over the soundtrack as an external (objective) narrator, in Fleishman's sense of that term.

"One cannot tell a story from the single point of view of one character in a film as one can in a novel," Graham Greene once explained. "You cannot look through the eyes of one character in a film." It is true that the central character remains on the screen more than anyone else in the movie, Greene continued, and his comments are often there on the soundtrack. "But we still don't see others completely from his point of view, as we do in the novel."

Therefore *Apocalypse Now* is robbed of some of the emotional intensity that one feels when one reads "Heart of Darkness," simply because in the book the narrator frequently communicates to the reader his subjective reaction to the episodes from the past he is narrating. For example, the filmgoer never grasps the extent to which Willard, the narrator of the film, is profoundly touched by Kurtz's tragedy in the movie, since many of the sage reflections about Kurtz's life and death which Marlow makes in the book are simply not in the film.

Apocalypse Now, when it finally reached the screen in 1979, turned out to be a mammoth spectacle, which Coppola shot almost entirely on location in the Philippines. As mentioned, the setting of the story is updated from the late Nineteenth Century to the time of the Vietnam War. As we know, Captain Benjamin Willard, played by Martin Sheen (*The Subject Was Roses*), who is the central character and narrator of the movie, is ordered by his superior officers to penetrate into the interior of the jungle and track down Col.

Walter E. Kurtz (Marlon Brando), a renegade officer who
has raised an army composed of deserters like himself and
of native tribesmen, in order to fight the war on his own
terms. When he locates Kurtz, Willard is to "terminate his
command with extreme prejudice," which is military jargon
meaning that Willard should assassinate Kurtz. Col. Kurtz, it
seems, rules over his followers like a fanatical war lord, and
has taken to employing brutal tactics to attain his objectives;
indeed, some of the atrocities Kurtz has committed have
sickened the members of the Army intelligence staff who
have succeeded in obtaining information about him.

Willard's first reaction to his mission is that liquidating
someone for killing people in wartime seems like "handing
out speeding tickets at the 'Indy 500.'" Besides, even though
Willard has been ordered to eliminate no less than six other
Vietnamese political undesirables in the recent past, this is
the first time his target has been an American and an officer. He therefore decides to withhold judgment about Kurtz
until he meets up with him personally.

As Willard chugs up the Mekong River in a river patrol
boat in search of Kurtz, film scholar Richard Blake comments, his journey becomes a symbolic voyage "backward
in time." Near the beginning of the trip Willard and the crew
of his small craft witness an air attack on a North
Vietnamese village carried out by Lieutenant Colonel
Kilgore (Robert Duvall), which utilizes all the facilities of
modern mechanized warfare, from helicopters and rockets
to radar-directed machine guns. By the time that Willard's
boat reaches Kurtz's compound in the heart of the dark jungle, the modern weaponry has been replaced by the
weapons of primitive man, as Kurtz's native followers, wear-
ing war paint, attack Willard's small vessel with arrows and
spears in an attempt to scare off the intruders. (The attack of
the natives is taken directly from the novel.) In entering
Kurtz's outpost in the wilderness, Willard has equivalently
stepped back into a lawless, prehistoric age where barbarism holds sway. The compound, then, becomes a graph-
ic visual metaphor which reflects Kurtz's gradual descent
into primitive barbarism.

In fact, the severed heads that lie scattered around the
grounds testify to the depths of pagan savagery to which
Kurtz has sunk during his sojourn in the jungle. The severed
heads, shown in long shot, recall the scene in the novel

when Marlow is shocked to see that Kurtz has shrunken heads stuck on pikes in front of his lodgings.

Furthermore, it is painfully clear to Willard that, despite the fact that Kurtz's native followers revere him as a god, Kurtz is incurably insane. Willard also discovers, when he at last meets Kurtz, that Kurtz is slowly dying of malaria; hence his physical illness is symbolic of his moral sickness.

When Kurtz takes Willard into custody, he is aware of the object of Willard's mission. "You are an errand boy," Kurtz scoffs, "sent by grocery clerks to collect the bill." Then Kurtz, in his malarial delirium, spends hours rambling to Willard about his theories of war and politics, which he maintains lie behind his becoming a rebel chieftain. Kurtz does this, not only because he wants a brother officer to hear his side of the story, but also because he ultimately wants Willard to explain to Kurtz's son his father's reasons for acting as he has. Significantly, even in the depths of his madness, Kurtz has not lost sight of the preciousness of family attachments. (Kurtz is not married in the novella, so Marlow goes to comfort Kurtz's fiancée, not his son, in the book, once he gets to Europe.)

In Kurtz's own mind, the ruthless tactics he has employed to prosecute his own private war represent in essence his unshakable conviction that the only way to conquer a cruel and inhuman enemy like the Vietcong is to become as cruel and inhuman as they are, and crush them by their own hideous methods.

By now Willard has definitely made up his mind to carry out his orders by killing Kurtz; and Kurtz, who has sensed from the beginning the reason why Willard was sent to find him, finally makes no effort to stop him. For one thing, Kurtz presumably prefers a quick death, as meted out by Willard, to a slow death from malaria. More importantly, as Willard explains in his voice-over commentary on the soundtrack, Kurtz wants to die bravely, like a soldier, at the hands of another soldier, and not be ignominiously butchered as a wretched renegade. Indeed, in order to die like a soldier, Kurtz dons his Green Beret uniform, while he is waiting for Willard to come and assassinate him. Willard accordingly enters Kurtz's murky lair and ceremoniously slays him with a machete. (Kurtz dies of natural causes in the book.)

Willard's killing of Kurtz is intercut with shots of the Cambodian tribe that is part of Kurtz's army slaughtering a sacrificial water buffalo, a scene which suggests that Willard implicitly sees his "execution" of the diabolical Kurtz for his hideous war crimes as a kind of ritual slaying. The ritual killing of the water buffalo, moreover, recalls an earlier sequence, set in Saigon, in which roast beef is served at a dinner, during which a general commissions Willard to assassinate Kurtz: "Fleshy roast beef is aggressively stabbed and cut" during the meal, writes Cahir in describing the scene. The stabbing of the roast beef, film scholar Louis Greiff observes, foreshadows the hacking up of the sacrificial water buffalo, which, in turn, parallels Willard's stabbing Kurtz to death with a machete.

After Willard has slain Kurtz, he pauses at Kurtz's desk and notices a typescript lying on it. We see in close-up that, scrawled in red across one page is the statement, "Drop the Bomb. Exterminate them all!" This is Kurtz's manner of indicating his way of ending the Vietnam War: he would like to have seen all of the North Vietnamese, soldiers and noncombatants alike, destroyed from the air. Col. Kurtz's cold-blooded remark recalls a similar passage in the novella, in which Marlow peruses a report which Kurtz had prepared for the International Society for the Suppression of Savage Customs. The report ends with a postscript, presumably added much later: "Exterminate the brutes."

When Willard leaves Kurtz's quarters, Kurtz's tribesmen submissively lay their weapons on the ground as he passes among them. Clearly they believe that the mantle of authority has passed from their deceased leader to the man he has allowed to slay him. But Willard, his mission accomplished, walks out of the compound and proceeds to the river bank, where his patrol boat awaits him to take him back to civilization.

As the boat pulls away from the shore, Willard hears the voice of Kurtz uttering the same phrase he had spoken just before he met his Maker: "The horror, the horror." At the end Kurtz was apparently vouchsafed a moment of lucidity, in which he realized what a depraved brute he had become. To Willard the phrase represents, as it does to Marlow in the novella, his own revulsion at the vicious inclination to evil he had seen revealed in Kurtz—a tendency that Kurtz had allowed to overpower his better nature and render him more savage by far than the enemy he was so intent on exterminating.

Hence the theme of the movie is the same as that of Conrad's novel. "In *Apocalypse Now,* just as in 'Heart of Darkness,' the central journey is both a literal and a metaphoric one," writes Joy Gould Boyum;[2] it is fundamentally "a voyage of discovery into the dark heart of man, and an encounter with his capacity for evil." In harmony with this observation, Coppola says that he too sees Willard's journey upriver as a metaphor for "the voyage of life that each of us takes within ourselves and during which we choose between good and evil."

Although some critics found those scenes in which Kurtz theorizes about the motivation for his unspeakable behavior wordy and overlong, most agreed that the movie contains some of the most extraordinary combat footage ever filmed. The battle scene that particularly stands out is the one in which the officer who is aptly named Kilgore systematically wipes out a strongly fortified enemy village from the air.

Kilgore, all decked out with a Stetson and gold neckerchief, looks as if he should be leading a cavalry charge rather than a helicopter attack. His fleet of helicopters is equipped with loudspeakers that blare forth Wagner's thunderous "Ride of the Valkyries"[3] as the choppers fly over the target area. "Wagner scares the hell out of the natives," Kilgore tells Willard, who is observing the operation as a passenger in Kilgore's copter. As a napalm strike wreaks havoc and destruction on the village below, Kilgore exults, "I love the smell of napalm in the morning. It has the smell of victory." It is spectacular scenes like this one that have prompted some commentators on the film to rank *Apocalypse Now,* which won one of the two Grand Prizes awarded at the 1979 Cannes Film Festival, among the great war movies of all time. Moreover, this writer feels that the film can likewise be numbered among the major adaptations of Conrad to the screen.

---

2. in *Double Exposure: Fiction into Film,* New York: New American Library, 1985
3. In Richard Wagner's opera *Die Walküre,* the Valkyries are the Norse god Odin's handmaidens who conduct the souls of the slain to Valhalla, where Odin receives them.

The Complex Morality of *Lord Jim*

R.A. Gekoski

R.A. Gekoski analyzes Marlow's—and by extension, the reader's—moral dilemma by analyzing the criteria for judging Jim's failure. Gekoski observes that Jim is guilty when judged by the simple standards of civil social interaction. But Marlow feels sympathy for Jim when he considers Jim's behavior in light of the circumstances, Jim's motives, his romantic nature, and his stature as an ordinary man, "one of us." Gekoski concludes that both interpretations of Jim's fate are true and reflect the complexity of the real moral world. R.A. Gekoski attended Oxford University, where he studied literature and wrote his doctoral thesis on Joseph Conrad.

Lord Jim is yet another trip into the 'heart of darkness', and once again deals with a romantic idealist whose dreams are shattered, yet who goes on to seek, and ambiguously to win, a final redemption at death. But Jim, though he shares certain qualities with both Peter Willems and Mr Kurtz,[1] is a further development in Conrad's maturing use of the hero. Jim is neither a petty scoundrel, like Willems, nor a degraded genius, like Kurtz; he is the first of a series of Conrad's 'simple and sensitive' protagonists: he is 'one of us'. . . .

As Jim is a different kind of character from Kurtz, so too is the Marlow of *Lord Jim* a changed man from the Marlow of 'Heart of Darkness'; superficially, he is the same teller of 'inconclusive' tales, but there is a crucial difference between the 'inconclusive' nature of 'Heart of Darkness' and that of *Lord Jim*. Although 'Heart of Darkness' ends with an ambiguous tension between its vision of the 'hollow' Kurtz, 'grubbing for ivory in the wretched bush', and the 'remarkable' Kurtz,

---

1. Willems from *An Outcast of the Islands* and Kurtz from 'Heart of Darkness'

Excerpted from R.A. Gekoski, *The Moral World of the Novelist* (London: Paul Elek, 1978). Copyright © 1978 by R.A. Gekoski. Reprinted by permission of the author.

who achieves a 'moral victory', nevertheless Marlow tells the tale from an assured, perhaps even an enlightened (he is constantly associated with images of the Buddha), point of view: he is relating something that he has learned. In *Lord Jim*, however, Marlow has none of this self-assurance: he wavers, changes his mind, contradicts himself, compulsively seeks out advice and guidance, and seems uncertain of the 'lesson' lurking ambiguously in his material. . . .

JUDGING JIM'S BEHAVIOR

Jim's failure on board the *Patna* has its inevitable consequences: his certificate is cancelled, and he is left to face his disgrace and ruin. But the moral problems that his experience brings to the fore are generally lost on him, for he is too intimately involved in his disgrace to be interested in the implications of his moral failure. Thus Conrad returns to using Marlow as a commentator on the causes, effects, and possible interpretations of Jim's allegedly cowardly behaviour. During the course of his careful analysis of Jim's history (most of Part I of the novel), Marlow is exposed to a vision of man's fate which threatens to overwhelm his previous allegiance to the 'few simple notions' that form the basis of human social interaction. Just as Jim's idealized conception of himself is tried by the nightmarish quality of his experience on board the *Patna*, so too are Marlow's simple ideals of human conduct tested by his mature understanding of the implications of Jim's jump. . . .

What Marlow sees during this momentary peep out of the shell is enough to change his opinion about the nature of things:

> It seemed to me I was being made to comprehend the Inconceivable—and I know of nothing to compare with the discomfort of such a sensation. I was made to look at the convention that lurks in all truth and on the essential sincerity of falsehood . . . as if the obscure truth involved were momentous enough to affect mankind's conception of itself.

It is altogether too easy to read this passage superficially, to miss the import of the phrase 'the convention that lurks in all truth and on the essential sincerity of falsehood'. It seems that 'truth' is merely an agreed formula, of no intrinsic importance, and that what we reject as 'falsehood' may, however base the action in which it issues, arise from motives of no mean kind.

This postulates a universe in which the basic fact is not human solidarity, but human loneliness:

> It is when we try to grapple with another man's intimate need that we perceive how incomprehensible, wavering, and misty are the beings that share with us the sight of the stars and the warmth of the sun. It is as if loneliness were a hard and absolute condition of existence; the envelope of flesh and blood on which our eyes are fixed melts before the out-stretched hand, and there remains only the capricious, unconsolable, and elusive spirit that no eye can follow, no hand can grasp.

We thus have two starkly contrasted views of reality: there is the everyday world, associated with light, words, and 'a few simple notions'; underlying that 'conventional' world, how-ever, a 'deeper' reality exists, associated with darkness, lone-liness, and absolute egoism. *Lord Jim* suggests that moral culpability exists only in the first of them. . . .

CIRCUMSTANCES AND MOTIVES

The thoughts triggered by Jim's jump imaginatively reveal to Marlow a reality different from, and deeper than, the real-ity of his everyday world. At which point, the question of Jim's guilt takes on new dimensions. Only if we are sure of our standards can we confidently judge transgression. If, as our deepest truth, we substitute an idea of man's ultimate loneliness and alienation from other human beings, for our previous ideal of human solidarity based on '*les valeurs idéales*',[2] then all concepts of human responsibility are changed. This accounts—in a schematic way—for Marlow's confused attitude to Jim.

If we re-examine the circumstances of Jim's jump in this light, he becomes much more sympathetic to us. At the most superficial level, it is necessary to remember the mitigating circumstances of his failure. Unlike the other officers of the *Patna*, Jim's first impulse is not simply to save his own skin; his paralysis is at least partially due to the hopelessness of the situation: the bulkheads cannot fail to burst, any alarm will produce a stampede amongst the pilgrims, there are far too few lifeboats, and a squall is moving quickly towards the *Patna*. The ship simply must sink at any moment. It seems as if Jim's choice is only whether eight hundred pilgrims will drown, or eight hundred pilgrims and himself. Even so,

2. ideal standards of merit

Jim might have stayed on board had not circumstances ironically contrived against him. Mistaking the cries of the
unworthy Captain and his officers as pleas for him to join
them in their lifeboat, he finally jumps. But the jump itself is
not willed, it simply happens: 'I had jumped . . . It seems.' It
seems more appropriate to say that Jim 'is jumped'. Furthermore, while the other officers of the *Patna* make their
escape upon learning that the ship did not sink, Jim stays to
face the consequences of his action. Thus his behaviour,
while impossible to condone, is nevertheless easy to sympathize with.

Conrad goes further, introducing deeper reasons to lessen
Jim's disgrace. The first of these lies in Marlow's vision of
universal loneliness, in which there is the clear implication
that, in the last analysis, one's duties are to one's self. This is
not to imply that they should be—they should not—but simply that they are. The phrase 'in the last analysis', as it is
used here, indicates why Conrad was so deeply suspicious of
'ideas' and 'Imagination': both tend to reveal unpleasant,
and corrosive, truths. Even the French Lieutenant whom
Marlow meets is inclined to admit the universality of cowardice: the primitive urge to save one's skin. This may explain Jim's having passively found himself in the water,
rather than actively jumping, as if an unconscious life-force
had exerted itself on his behalf.

Once we recognize this instinct of self-preservation, and
the way in which it isolates the individual in moments of crisis, then a second factor emerges to illuminate Jim's history.
According to conventional notions of duty and honour, Jim
is as guilty as are the other officers of the *Patna;* such is the
inevitable verdict of the Court of Inquiry, which cancels the
certificates of all the officers. But just as Kurtz may be of
greater stature than the 'pilgrims' and 'flabby devils' of
'Heart of Darkness' (though his crime is greater than theirs),
so too is Jim a man and not a fool. It is men like Jim, who is
'one of us', who remind us that we are all (at least potentially) guilty, that any of us might jump from some *Patna.* In
judging him, we must accept that we judge ourselves. No
consideration is likelier to lead to a lenient verdict.

The third factor in the re-examination of Jim's case lies in
the possibility of atonement on his part. Jim, unlike the other
officers of the *Patna,* both accepts and believes in the standards by which he is judged. His character could hardly be

JIM'S JUMP FROM THE *PATNA*

In the following excerpt from Lord Jim, *Marlow listens to Jim explain how he jumped ship in the storm. Jim hears men already in a lifeboat call to a sailor named George and finds himself responding to their call. Marlow sympathizes silently.*

"I could hear them knocking about, down there, and a voice as if crying up a shaft called out 'George'. Then three voices together raised a yell. They came to me separately: one bleated, another screamed, one howled. Ough!". . .

There was a suggestion of awful stillness in his face, in his movements, in his very voice when he said "They shouted"— and involuntarily I pricked up my ears for the ghost of that shout that would be heard directly through the false effect of silence. "There were eight hundred people in that ship," he said, impaling me to the back of my seat with that awful blank stare. "Eight hundred living people, and they were yelling after the one dead man to come down and be saved. 'Jump, George! Jump! Oh, jump!' I stood by with my hand on the davit. I was very quiet. It had come over pitch dark. You could see neither sky nor sea. I heard the boat alongside go bump, bump, and not another sound down there for a while, but the ship under me was full of talking noises. Suddenly the skipper howled, 'Mein Gott! The squall! The squall! Shove off!' With the first hiss of rain, and the first gust of wind, they screamed, 'Jump, George! We'll catch you! Jump!' The ship began a slow plunge; the rain swept over her like a broken sea; my cap flew off my head; my breath was driven back into my throat. I heard as if I had been on the top of a tower another wild screech, 'Geo-o-o-orge! Oh, jump!' She was going down, down, head first under me.". . .

"I had jumped . . ." He checked himself, averted his gaze . . . "It seems," he added. . . .

You had to listen to him as you would to a small boy in trouble. He didn't know. It had happened somehow. It would never happen again. He had landed partly on somebody and fallen across a thwart. He felt as though all his ribs on his left side must be broken; then he rolled over, and saw vaguely the ship he had deserted uprising above him, with the red sidelight glowing large in the rain like a fire on the brow of a hill seen through a mist. "She seemed higher than a wall; she loomed like a cliff over the boat . . . I wished I could die," he cried. "There was no going back. It was as if I had jumped into a well—into an everlasting deep hole . . ."

Joseph Conrad, *Lord Jim*, 1900.

called irretrievably corrupt. His motives, like those of Kurtz, are essentially those of an 'idealised selfishness', but could not be called wicked. Following his trial, Jim is obsessed with the thought that he may never get a chance to atone for his behaviour, never be able to realize the ideal picture of himself that he cannot abandon. Marlow is far from sympathetic to this aspect of him ('the idea obtrudes itself that he made so much of his disgrace, while it is the guilt alone that matters') but nevertheless he, too, ponders the possibility of some redemptive experience for Jim. Although Jim has twice been betrayed—and become a betrayer—through his romantic self-glorification, he retains his belief that he needs but one more chance to prove his value. The second half of the novel, in which Jim becomes Lord Jim, is the chronicle of that chance.

Before proceeding to a brief discussion of the Patusan episode, let us look once more at the possible mitigating factors that lead us to view Jim in a sympathetic light. Although Conrad is sensitive to the ambiguities exposed by Jim's betrayal, he nevertheless does not wish absolutely to condone Jim's behaviour. Far from it. Having established the standard necessary to social cohesion ('we exist only insofar as we hang together'), and having revealed, through the implications of Jim's failure, a deeper view of reality in which Jim cannot be said to be in any way unique in his failure, Conrad uses Part I of *Lord Jim* to expose Marlow (and the reader) to a variety of possible points of view on Jim's story. These are modulated so that Marlow (and the reader) continue to vacillate between outright condemnation of Jim and the desire to excuse him. . . .

JIM IS SENT TO PATUSAN

Part II of *Lord Jim* attempts to supply an answer to the apparently insurmountable difficulties set up by the clash between man's fundamental egoism and the imperative to 'hang together'. Jim is sent to Patusan by Marlow's friend Stein, to head an obscure trading station. Stein, as interested in specimens of humanity as he is in his rare and beautiful collection of butterflies, gives an immediate diagnosis of Jim's character: '"He is romantic—romantic," he repeated. "And that is very bad, very bad . . . Very good, too," he added.' . . .

Coming to Patusan at a time of disorder and factional dispute, the determined and courageous Jim uses his allegiance with the chief Doramin to establish a peaceful and prosperous community. Taking the Eurasian girl Jewel as his mistress, he becomes the adored leader of the land; unlike Mr Kurtz, however, he is a beneficent deity. When a band of starving desperadoes, led by the notorious Gentleman Brown, descends upon Patusan and is quickly driven on to the defensive, Jim arranges a meeting with Brown, who seems to assess Jim's character in a flash: 'And there ran through the rough talk a vein of subtle reference to their common blood, an assumption of common experience; a sickening suggestion of common guilt, of secret knowledge that was like a bond of their minds and of their hearts.' Jim finds it impossible to resist, and instead of ordering the immediate slaughter of Brown and his men, allows them safe passage back to the sea. Guided by the spiteful Portuguese Cornelius, whose position (and daughter) have been usurped by Jim, the outlaws ambush and murder a large party of natives led by Doramin's son. Jim, who had previously pledged his life for the safety of the community, walks proudly to Doramin's hut, where he is summarily shot.

It is not hard to understand the moral dilemma that Gentleman Brown thrusts upon Jim. With regard to the safety of the inhabitants of Patusan, it would no doubt have been expedient to murder Brown and his bloodthirsty followers. On the other hand, Jim could neither foresee the treachery of Cornelius, nor the circumstances leading inexorably to the ambush of the native party. Further, he is more than superficially aware that men can act basely without being themselves wicked: 'Men act badly sometimes without being much worse than others'. Brown is irredeemably bad, thoroughly corrupt, but Jim could hardly be expected to know this; his decision to give Brown the same chance that he had himself sought cannot but be admired. It seems to me that, on balance, Jim is right to let Brown make his escape. Moral decisions must not be judged in terms of their unforeseen consequences: had Brown and his followers simply made their exit without bloodshed, there could have been no good reason to assert that Jim had acted foolishly. Assuming Jim's choice to have been the correct one, we are left with the paradox that his jump from the *Patna* was a moral failure from which he attempted (in his own mind) to evade responsibility, while his decision with regard to Gentleman Brown was a moral triumph for which he nevertheless accepted punishment. There seems little doubt that Jim had made the most of that 'second chance' (actually it is a third chance) for which he had yearned. Marlow is, at times, sure that this is true. . . .

AMBIGUITY SURROUNDS JIM'S DEATH

Following their last meeting, Marlow is convinced that Jim 'had at last mastered his fate'. Perhaps Jim has 'mastered his fate', but his attitude when confronting the death that it is his responsibility to accept is far from humble. There is no doubt that the language used to describe Jim's last minutes leads one to view his death as only ambiguously redemptive; as Jim leaves his faithful servant Tamb' Itam: ' "Nothing can touch me," he said in a last flicker of superb egoism.' Jim leaves Tamb' Itam and Jewel, and walks confidently up the hill to Doramin's to meet his death: 'They say that the white man sent right and left at all those faces a proud and unflinching glance. Then with his hand over his lips he fell forward, dead.' Marlow's final words seem to convey to us both possible interpretations of Jim's death: that he had died in a redemptive act of self-sacrifice, and that he was the same supreme egoist to the very last. . . .

We seem to have two possible and apparently contradictory interpretations of Jim's fate. But there is no need to choose between them: they are both true. In forging for himself the character of Lord Jim, Jim has successfully managed to unite what had previously been felt (by everyone except Stein) to be the incompatible demands of his fierce egoism and his social responsibilities. In 'following his dream' he remained at the level of consciousness that destroyed Mr Kurtz, but fortunately his dream was not incompatible with ordinary moral conventions, as was Kurtz's. Quite the opposite: Jim is 'one of us', his egoism is firmly grounded in accepted moral standards, his dreams of glory are not only not incompatible with the fulfilment of his moral duties, they absolutely demand it.

The everyday reality of 'hanging together' through our 'few simple notions', and the underlying reality of loneliness and absolute egoism, are often in conflict, so much so that the conflict itself should not be thought about. But Jim is fortunate in that the promptings of his 'own particular devil' are compatible with what society demands of him. He is thus able, at the end, to make a satisfactory, but not general-

158 Readings on Joseph Conrad

izable, synthesis between the entirely self-regarding demands of the naked ego and the entirely other-regarding demands of society. This is why Stein told Marlow that it might be 'very good' to be romantic; just as Part I of *Lord Jim* assesses the 'very bad' aspects of Jim's romanticism, so does Part II redress the balance (though less convincingly). Such an interpretation of the second half of *Lord Jim* helps us to account for what seems the paradoxical nature of Jim's feelings for the people of Patusan: 'he seemed to love the land and the people with a sort of fierce egoism, with a contemptuous tenderness.' Jim's love and tenderness are, in the final analysis, self-regarding—but love and tenderness, even as expressions of one's essential selfishness, are not contemptible emotions.

CHAPTER 4

Conrad's Novels After 1900

Imperialism and Capitalism in *Nostromo*

Robert Penn Warren

Robert Penn Warren describes *Nostromo* as Conrad's vision of imperialism and capitalism. Warren explains that each character represents an idea; for example, Nostromo represents selfishness and Mrs. Gould represents commitment to an ideal. Near the end, the ideal vision of imperialism and capitalism is shattered with Mrs. Gould's realization that wealth may be accursed and with the symbolic dark clouds forming on the horizon. Robert Penn Warren, American novelist, poet, and critic, taught at the University of Minnesota and at Yale University. He is the author of numerous books, among them the novels *All the King's Men* and *The World Enough and Time*, and the critical works *Understanding Poetry* and *Understanding Fiction*. He was twice awarded the Pulitzer Prize.

Early in 1903, from Pent Farm, which he had rented from Ford Madox Ford, Joseph Conrad wrote to John Galsworthy: "Only with my head full of a story, I have not been able to write a single word–except the title, which shall be, I think: *Nostromo*." On July 8 of the same year, he wrote to R.B. Cunninghame Graham: "I am dying over that cursed *Nostromo* thing. All my memories of Central America seem to slip away. I just had a glimpse 25 years ago,—a short glance.". . . Then on September 1 of 1904, in a letter to Galsworthy, came the cry of triumph: "Finished! Finished! on the 30th in Hope's house in Stanford in Essex." Three days later, in a letter to William Rothenstein, the note of triumph has faded away:

> What the book is like, I don't know. I don't suppose it'll damage me: but I know that it is open to much intelligent criticism. For the other sort I don't care. Personally, I am not satisfied. It

is something—but not *the* thing I tried for. There is no exul-
tation, none of the temporary sense of achievement which is
so soothing. . . .

In this book Conrad endeavored to create a great, massive, multiphase symbol that would render his total vision of
the world, his sense of individual destiny, his sense of man's
place in nature, his sense of history and society.

A COMPLEX PLOT

First, *Nostromo* is a complex of personal stories, intimately
interfused, a chromatic scale of attitudes, a study in the definition and necessity of "illusion" as Conrad freighted that
word. Each character lives by his necessary idealization, up
the scale from the "natural" man Nostromo, whose only idealization is that primitive one of his vanity, to Emilia Gould,
who, more than any other, has purged the self and entered
the human community.

The personal stories are related not only in the contact of
person and person in plot and as carriers of variations of the
theme of illusion, but also in reference to the social and historical theme. That is, each character is also a carrier of an
attitude toward, a point of view about, society; and each is an
actor in a crucial historical moment. This historical moment
is presumably intended to embody the main issues of
Conrad's time: capitalism, imperialism, revolution, social
justice. Many of the personal illusions bear quite directly on
these topics: Viola's libertarianism, with its dignity and leo-
nine self-sufficiency and, even, contempt for the mob;
Charles Gould's obsession in his mission; Avellanos's liberalism and Antonia's patriotic piety; Holroyd's concern with a
"pure form of Christianity" which serves as a mask and justification for his imperialistic thirst for power; even the pos-
turing and strutting "Caesarism" of Pedrito Montero, whose
imagination had been inflamed by reading third-rate historical novels.

A DIFFERENT VIEW OF IMPERIALISM

All readers of Conrad know the classic picture of imperialism at its brutal worst in "Heart of Darkness," the degradation and insanity of the process, and remember the passage
spoken by Marlow:

> The conquest of the earth, which mostly means the taking it
> away from those who have a different complexion or slightly

flatter noses than ourselves, is not a pretty thing when you look into it too much. What redeems it is the idea only.

In "Heart of Darkness" we see the process absolutely devoid of "idea," with lust, sadism, and greed rampant. In *Nostromo* we see the imperialistic process in another perspective, as the bringer of order and law to a lawless land, of prosperity to a land of grinding poverty. At least, that is the perspective in which Charles Gould sees himself and his mine:

> What is wanted here is law, good faith, order, security. Anyone can declaim about these things, but I pin my faith to material interests. Only let the material interests once get a firm footing, and they are bound to impose the conditions on which alone they can continue to exist. That's how your money-making is justified here in the face of lawlessness and disorder. It is justified because the security which it demands must be shared with an oppressed people.

This passage and Gould's conception of his own role may be taken as the central fact of the social and historical theme of *Nostromo*. But how does Conrad intend us to regard this passage? Albert Guerard, Jr., in his careful and brilliant study of Conrad, says that the mine "corrupts Sulaco, bringing civil war rather than progress." That strikes me as far too simple. There has been a civil war, but the forces of "progress"—i.e., the San Tomé mine and the capitalistic order—have won. And we must admit that the society at the end of the book is preferable to that at the beginning.

THE IRONY OF GOULD AND HIS VICTORY

Charles Gould's statement, and his victory, are, however, hedged about with all sorts of ironies. For one thing—and how cunning is this stroke!—there is Decoud's narrative, the letter written to his sister in the midst of the violence, that appears at the very center of the book; and the voice of the sceptic tells us how history is fulfilled. For another thing—and this stroke is even more cunning—old Captain Mitchell, faithful-hearted and stupid, the courageous dolt, is the narrator of what he pleases to call the "historical events." His is the first human voice we have heard, in Chapter II of Part I, after the mists part to exhibit the great panorama of the mountains, campo,[1] city, and gulf; and in Chapter X of Part III, just after Nostromo has made his decision to ride to Cayta and save the Concession and the new state, the voice

---

1. a large grassy plain in South America

of Captain Mitchell resumes. He is speaking long afterwards, to some nameless distinguished visitor, and now all
the violence and passion and the great anonymous forces of
history come under the unconscious irony of his droning
anecdotes. We can say of Captain Mitchell what Conrad says
of Pedrito Montero, inflamed by his bad novels read in a
Parisian garret: his mind is "wrapped . . . in the futilities of
historical anecdote." Captain Mitchell's view is, we may say,
the "official view": "Progress" has triumphed, the world has
achieved itself, there is nothing left but to enjoy the fruits of
the famous victory. Thus the very personalities of the narrators function as commentary (in a triumph of technical virtuosity) as their voices are interpolated into Conrad's high
and impersonal discourse.

But we do not have to depend merely on this subtle commentary. Toward the end of the book, at a moment of pause
when all seems to be achieved on a sort of Fiddler's Green at
the end of history, a party has gathered in the garden of the
Casa Gould. They discuss in a desultory way the possibility
of a new revolution, and the existence of secret societies in
which Nostromo, despite his secret treasure and growing
wealth, is a great force. Emilia Gould demands: "Will there
never be any peace?" And Dr. Monygham replies:

> There is no peace and no rest in the development of material
> interests. They have their law, and their justice. But it is
> founded on expediency, and is inhuman; it is without recti-
> tude, and without the continuity and force that can be found
> only in a moral principle. Mrs. Gould, the time approaches
> when all that the Gould Concession stands for shall weigh as
> heavily upon the people as the barbarism, cruelty, and mis-
> rule of a few years back.

The material interests have fulfilled their historical mission, or are in the process of fulfilling it. Even Charles
Gould, long before, in defining his mission to bring order
through the capitalistic development, had not seen that
order as the end, only as a phase. He had said: "A better justice will come afterwards. That's our ray of hope." And in
this connection we may recall in *Under Western Eyes* how,
after hearing the old teacher of languages give his disillusioned view of revolution, Miss Haldin can still say: "I would
take liberty from any hand as a hungry man would snatch at
a piece of bread. The true progress must begin after." In
other words, the empire-builder and hard-bitten realist
Gould and the idealistic girl join to see beyond the era of

material interests and the era of revolution the time of "true progress" and the "better justice." Somewhere, beyond, there will be, according to Miss Haldin's version, the period of concord:

> I believe that the future will be merciful to us all. Revolutionist and reactionary, victim and executioner, betrayer and betrayed, they shall all be pitied together when the light breaks on our black sky at last. Pitied and forgotten; for without that there can be no union and no love.

Emilia Gould, trapped in her "merciless nightmare" in the "Treasure House of the World," leans over the dying Capataz and hears him say, "But there is something accursed in wealth," and then begins to tell her where the treasure is hidden. And she bursts out: "Let it be lost for ever." Symbolically, this is her moment of vision, her repudiation of the logic of material interests.

If in this moment of vision, Emilia Gould and (in a sense that we shall come to) Conrad himself repudiate the material interests as merely a step toward justice, what are we to make of revolution? We may remember that Conrad most anxiously meditated the epigraphs of his various books, and that the epigraph of *Nostromo* is the line from Shakespeare: "So foul a sky clears not without a storm." It is innocent to think that this refers merely to the "storm" which is the action of the novel, the revolution that has established the order of material interests in Sulaco. If the sky has cleared at the end of that episode, even now in the new peace we see, as Dr. Monygham sees, the blacker and more terrible thunderheads piling up on the far horizon.

DARKNESS FOLLOWS VICTORY

"Heart of Darkness" and *Nostromo* are, in one sense, an analysis and unmasking of capitalism as it manifested itself in the imperialistic adventure. Necessarily this involves the topic of revolution. The end of *Nostromo* leaves the sky again foul, and in the years immediately after finishing that novel Conrad turns to two studies of revolution, *The Secret Agent*, begun in 1905 and published in 1907, and *Under Western Eyes*, begun in 1908 and published in 1911. These books are in their way an analysis and unmasking of revolution to correspond to the already accomplished analysis and unmasking of capitalism and imperialism. In the world of revolution we find the same complex egotism, vanity, violence, and even noble illusion. As the old teacher of languages in *Under Western Eyes* puts it:

> A violent revolution falls into the hands of the narrow-minded fanatics and of tyrannical hypocrites at first. Afterwards comes the turn of all the pretentious intellectual failures of the time. Such are the chiefs and the leaders. You will notice that I have left out the mere rogues. The scrupulous and the just, the noble, humane, and devoted natures; the unselfish and the intelligent may begin a movement—but it passes away from them. They are not the leaders of a revolution. They are its victims: the victims of disgust, of disenchantment—often of remorse. Hopes grotesquely betrayed, ideals caricatured—that is the definition of revolutionary success. There have been in every revolution hearts broken by such successes.

We could take this, in appropriate paraphrase, as a summary of the situation at the end of *Nostromo*. There is the same irony of success. There has been the same contamination of the vision in the very effort to realize the vision. As Emilia Gould reflects: "There was something inherent in the necessities of successful action which carried with it the moral degradation of the idea."

Irony in *The Secret Agent*

E.M.W. Tillyard

E.M.W. Tillyard argues that the irony in *The Secret Agent* contributes to the novel's humor and coherence. Tillyard cites the ironic situations connected with Verloc's hat, the mild irony in discussions of Mrs. Verloc's marginal intelligence, and the irony of plans and expectations that go awry. Though Tillyard acknowledges faults in the novel, he thinks its engaging story makes them hardly noticeable. E.M.W. Tillyard is the author of *The Epic Strain in the English Novel* and critical works on Milton and Shakespeare.

Responses to Conrad's *Secret Agent* have ranged from total capitulation to coolish approval. . . . I can only concur in most of the praise that writers have bestowed on Conrad's ironic method, on his success in keeping his dreadful story within the bounds of comedy. His prevailing ironic method is to make very large the distance between the way things appear to the persons in the story and the way they are made to appear to the reader.

THE THEME OF VERLOC'S HAT

The theme of Verloc's hat provides typical instances. Verloc's hat and heavy overcoat, constantly worn indoors, are powerful agents in building up Verloc's character; they are symbols of his physical and mental frowstiness. Then, rather more than half-way through the book, Conrad gives us the reasons for Verloc's habit of retaining his clothing: 'It was not devotion to an outdoor life, but the frequentation of foreign cafés which was responsible for that habit, investing with a character of unceremonious impermanency Mr. Verloc's steady fidelity to his own fireside.' And of course Verloc has no notion of this discrepancy between appearance and reality. The culminating chapter containing the murder ends thus:

Excerpted from E.M.W. Tillyard, "*The Secret Agent* Reconsidered," *Essays in Criticism,* July 1961, pp. 309–19. Reprinted by permission of *Essays in Criticism.*

> Then all became still. Mrs. Verloc on reaching the door had
> stopped. A round hat disclosed in the middle of the floor by
> the moving of the table rocked slightly on its crown in the
> wind of her flight.

These words are perfect in deflating the murder—that is, as it
concerns the victim. The grotesque rocking of the inverted
bowler resembles and mocks Verloc's precarious state of
mind in the last weeks, just as its dethronement from the emi-
nence of his head duplicates and minimises his own down-
fall. The hat figures for the last time when Ossipon, now convinced that he is the victim of a plot to murder him, returns
with Winnie Verloc to the house in Brett Street. He is standing
in the shop looking through the glass of the door into the par-
lour, where Verloc lies, apparently asleep; Ossipon is still
under the illusion that he had been blown to pieces in
Greenwich Park:

> But the true sense of the scene he was beholding came to
> Ossipon through the contemplation of the hat. It seemed an
> extraordinary thing, an ominous object, a sign. Black and rim
> upward, it lay on the floor before the couch as if prepared to
> receive the contributions of pence from people who would
> come presently to behold Mr. Verloc in the fullness of his
> domestic ease reposing on a sofa.

There is, of course, more than one kind of irony here. For
instance, there is the contrast between the appearance of
domestic ease and the reality of its opposite. But the main
irony consists in the fantastic distance between what Conrad
instructs the reader to think of, the likeness of the hat to a
beggar's inviting coins, and Ossipon's vision of it as a symbol of chaos come again. And by achieving that distance
Conrad makes the reader very happy indeed.

Mrs. Verloc

Further, Conrad is tactful in his use of this ironic tool. Winnie
Verloc is pathetic and even noble. It would be a piece of very
bad taste to submit her to the kind and the degree of ridicule
that is apt for her husband. Nevertheless, she cannot be
allowed to engage our sympathies too seriously, or the whole
tone of the book will be ruined. So in the murder scene,
where her sufferings are great, Conrad avoids irony as far as
she is concerned and concentrates on reducing the scale of
the potentially tragic action. Before the scene he had kept on
insisting that her view into things did not go deep, as when he
tells us that 'Mrs. Verloc wasted no portion of this transient life

in seeking for fundamental information'. And this insistence is continued into the scene itself with such remarks as 'The visions of Mrs. Verloc lacked nobility and magnificence.' She is indeed a woman with small range of mind, incapable of holding more than one important thing in it at the same time. Hatred of Verloc as the murderer of Stevie at first quite usurps it, to be expelled by her use of the carving-knife. Then the vision of the gallows takes complete possession. In her extremity she is too ignorant to know how to escape abroad. By such means Conrad succeeds in rendering innocuous the powerful sympathies the reader might have had with her obsessive devotion to her helpless brother. And that devotion too had come in for its share of criticism before the catastrophe, for it is a short-sighted devotion, quite preventing Winnie from seeing why her mother had left Brett Street for the almshouse. Thus Conrad contrives to deflate Mrs. Verloc, but without the impropriety of an ironic deflation. He does something similar before her suicide, which in its turn must not be allowed to cross the borderline into tragedy. The scene that follows Mrs. Verloc's flight from her house and her accidental encounter with Ossipon is both macabre and richly comic. And the comedy is that of cross purposes and mutual misunderstanding. Thinking that it is Verloc who was blown up and ignorant of the murder, Ossipon at first believes that Winnie is a genuine pick-up, a windfall, and prepares to make use of his good luck. But he soon sees he is wrong and flies to the opposite error of diagnosing her as a homicidal maniac, from whom at all costs he must escape. Conrad is able, and without impropriety, to include Winnie in the comic context and in so doing to spotlight her stupidity. The climax comes when, waiting for the Southampton train to leave, she misinterprets Ossipon's words about Stevie (Comrade Ossipon, it will be remembered, was a devoted student of Cesare Lombroso and his theory of the 'criminal type'):

> 'He was an extraordinary lad, that brother of yours. Most interesting to study. A perfect type in a way. Perfect.'
>
> He spoke scientifically in his secret fear. And Mrs. Verloc, hearing these words of commendation vouchsafed to her beloved dead, swayed forward with a flicker of light in her sombre eyes, like a ray of sunshine heralding a tempest of rain.
>
> 'He was that indeed,' she whispered, softly, with quivering lips. 'You took a lot of notice of him, Tom. I loved you for it.'

After Mrs. Verloc has reached that degree of stupidity, of total grossness of misapprehension, we cannot think of her suicide as a tragic event.

THE IRONY OF PLANS AND EXPECTATIONS

But the *Secret Agent* is pervaded by another kind of irony, and one which, like the first kind, helps towards making the book a unity. It is the irony of great plans having trivial results and of the weightiest results being effected by trivial means. It is the kind of irony that encourages men to keep their eyes open and not to expect too much logic and tidiness from life. . . .

The first hint of expectations being falsified occurs in the opening scene at the (German or Austrian?) Embassy. There, Privy Councillor Wurmt questions the vigilance of the English police, but the vigilance turns out to be embarrassingly greater than he had ever expected. Later, in the same scene, Vladimir announces that England must be brought into line with the Continent in the way she deals with revolutionaries: in the end his action only helps to perpetuate the difference of methods. Chief Inspector Heat hopes to use the explosion of the bomb to justify the imprisonment of Michaelis, whom he dislikes seeing at large; but this dislike awakens the suspicions of his superior and leads to a rebuff. The domestic set-up of the Verlocs is a humble and small-scale affair, yet it makes itself felt in embassies and offices of state; while in turn the feelings thus aroused there are destined to lead nowhere. The mother of Mrs. Verloc, thinking that her presence in the Brett Street house may ultimately annoy Mr. Verloc and finally lead to his turning against her mentally deficient son, heroically contrives to retire to an almshouse. Her act is rich in unforeseen consequences. It leads first to Mr. Verloc's taking more notice of Stevie and finally to his using him to deposit the bomb that blows Stevie up, and second to Winnie's sewing the address of the house under Stevie's coat-collar, an act which identifies him as the blown-up man. Mrs. Verloc did another thing to help Stevie. She joined with her daughter in impressing on him the measureless 'goodness' of Mr. Verloc. Thus impressed they thought he would be more docile in Mr. Verloc's presence and hence more acceptable. It was through Stevie's blindly loyal belief in this 'goodness' that he let himself be persuaded to carry the bomb and so meet his death. The Assistant Commissioner of

Police hoped that the Greenwich explosion might become a *cause célèbre*[1] and show up the iniquities of foreign embassies; and immediately, with Verloc's death, it lapsed into impenetrable obscurity. Most obvious of all, Verloc's efforts to pacify Winnie over Stevie's death serve instead to enrage her into committing murder. And lastly there is Ossipon, whose exposure to the same process is the *coda*[2] of the novel. Ossipon, as well as affecting to be a revolutionary, was the *gigolo*[3] of a steady succession of mature women not without means. He expected Winnie Verloc, widow of a man obviously possessed of means, to take her place in the succession. Finding her a murderess and haunted by the horror of her end, he is put off women altogether and takes to drink instead. I have questioned the motivation of this part of the novel, but in ironic idea it is strictly in accord with the rest. Thus, the theme of ends miscarrying goes right through and can hardly not have been intended by its author to be a means towards unity of impression. . . .

IRONY SUSPENDED FOR THE ASSISTANT COMMISSIONER

Conrad suspends his ironic method in dealing with the Assistant Commissioner and perhaps also with the Home Secretary.

As first presented, the Assistant Commissioner might well be within the scope of Conrad's ironic method:

> At headquarters the Chief Inspector was admitted at once to the Assistant Commissioner's private room. He found him, pen in hand, bent over a great table bestrewn with papers, as if worshipping an enormous double inkstand of bronze and crystal. Speaking tubes resembling snakes were tied by the heads to the back of the Assistant Commissioner's wooden armchair, and their gaping mouths seemed ready to bite his elbow.

Here we might easily think of the Commissioner as an unconscious Laocoön[4] caught in the coils of officialdom. But very soon we learn that he is as well aware of the coils as we are and as averse to them as Conrad would like his readers to be. The ironic distance between character and reader has been closed. Far from welcoming the sedentary imprisonment of administration, the Assistant Commissioner had an adventurous nature and would have preferred an active post

1. a sensational case taken up by the people   2. a passage that brings a piece to a close
3. a paid escort or companion   4. a Trojan priest of Apollo killed with his two sons by two sea serpents for having warned his people of the Trojan horse

in the tropics, such as he once had. He is denied his wish because, in a moment of blindness alien to his usual discriminating nature, he has married the wrong woman. Here is a perfect opportunity for the ironic method; but Conrad passes it by, allowing the Commissioner to have his own ironic situation quite under control:

> Chained to a desk in the thick of four millions of men, he considered himself the victim of an ironic fate—the same, no doubt, which had brought about his marriage with a woman exceptionally sensitive in the matter of colonial climate, besides other limitations testifying to the delicacy of her nature.

In fact, far from distancing him, Conrad creates in the Assistant Commissioner a man pretty close to himself. With the Home Secretary the case is slightly different. His physique and his clothes receive ironic treatment, presenting themselves to us and to himself differently, as when we learn that 'the eyes, with puffy lower lids, stared with a haughty droop on each side of a hooked, aggressive nose, nobly salient in the vast pale circumference of the face'. But there is nothing especially ironic in the way Conrad tells us how he coped with the problem presented to him by the Assistant Commissioner.

Another point. Not only does the Assistant Commissioner remain outside the area of Conrad's irony; he is the one person whose plans do not miscarry. True, he had hoped, as I have noted, that the Greenwich Park bomb would be the occasion of a *cause célèbre*, and his hopes were disappointed. But he scores substantial successes. He brings his subordinate to heel, as his two predecessors had failed to do; he had at last (in spite of his wife) been caught up in a job with a spice of adventure in it; and he managed to flatten Mr. Vladimir, whose methods of dealing with revolutionaries he abhorred. Conrad dismisses him with, 'he had had a full evening.' He might with equal truth have added, 'and a very successful day'.

A SIMPLE IRONIC TALE EXPANDED

These matters, little touched on by the critics, have their bearing on the better-known dispute as to whether or not the police scenes are integrated with the rest, which is almost identical with the dispute about unity. . . .

The majestic scale of the scenes between the two police officers prompts a last doubt as to the perfection of the *Secret Agent*. Is not the scale of the separate scene-units perhaps too big for the general scale? Conrad called his novel 'a simple tale', and it is nothing of the kind. He may have meant it to be, but when it came to the execution he wove a complex plot and gave us some highly developed characters. More important, he worked through a series of massive, long-drawn-out scenes. It would be wrong to complain of the length of the culminating scene ending with the murder; but should it have been matched by scenes equally massive? Think of the long opening scene in the embassy, of the intricate sparring between Heat and his superior, of the cab drive from Brett Street to the almshouses. I believe that Conrad, intending a simple ironic tale, could not resist the urge to employ the technique of the long novel and so allowed the supporting incidents to acquire an excessive consequence.

The parts of the novel are so good that in the act of reading them we are not likely to be bothered with their disproportionate scale, or with their relation to the whole. . . . Then there *are* the various features making for unity that I mentioned in the first section of this essay; and these help powerfully to distract us from the novel's failings. It is only when we have ceased reading and look back and reflect on the whole that our doubts arise and we reach this conclusion: that with all its merits the *Secret Agent* hovers a little uneasily between a novel in the grand manner and the long short-story.

Symbolic Characters in *Victory*

Tony Tanner

Tony Tanner argues that the gentlemanly Heyst is vulnerable to the destructive gossip of Schomberg, the vicious goals of the antigentleman Mr. Jones, and the attractiveness of Lena. Tanner argues further that Heyst fails because he drifts detachedly while others act. Tony Tanner has taught at King's College in Cambridge, England, and lectured at Stanford University in California. He is the author of *Conrad's 'Lord Jim,'* *The Reign of Wonder,* and *The City of Words.*

There are two key words in *Victory,* 'gentleman' and 'gossip.' 'Gentleman' usually occurs in reference to Heyst or Mr Jones, but it is deployed in a wide variety of conversations and issues from many different mouths. To gain some deeper sense of what Conrad might have been about in making this word both 'hollow' and central to his novel, it is worth reminding ourselves of the importance of that word in the latter part of the nineteenth century, particularly in England. . . .

A Mr. F. Lieber writing in 1847, put it this way:[1]

> The term Gentleman in its highest acceptation signifies that character which is distinguished by strict honour, self-possession, forbearance, generous as well as *refined* feelings, and polished deportment. . . . It seems to me that we always connect the ideas of honour, polish, collectedness of mind and liberal disposition with the word gentleman, and feel that its antagonistic characters are the clown, the *gossip,* the backbiter, the dullard, coward, braggart, fretter, swaggerer and bully. . . .

'Gossip'—the other key word—effectively destroys Heyst, his 'courtesy' being powerless against, and annihilated by, the gratuitous 'calumny' of others, mainly emanating from our old friend, or rather Conrad's old *bête noire,*[2] Schomberg.

1. in *Character of the Country Gentleman* 2. a disliked person; someone to avoid

Excerpted from Tony Tanner, "Gentlemen and Gossip: Aspects of Evolution and Language in Conrad's *Victory,*" Summer 1986. Reprinted by permission of the publisher, Manchester University Press.

The gentleman, and speech—these were considered two of the 'highest' products of evolution. And in their degraded, perverted, or 'scandalously' travestied forms—Mr Jones and Schomberg's gossip—they can destroy the higher, 'authentic' forms. 'Scandal' is another key word in the book—as it derives from *scandere,* to climb, and *skandalon,* a stumbling block—it appropriately conflates the idea of ascent and fall, and in one of its many ironic narrative developments, *Victory* does indeed re-enact the 'scandalous' fall of the most 'highly ascended' man; Heyst, Number One, the 'saviour', the namer of things and people (from the German *heissen*—to name), a second Adam, who is himself called many names—-'Enchanted Heyst', 'Hard Facts', the 'Spider', the 'Enemy', the 'Hermit'—but succumbs to the slanderous and malicious mal-naming of him by Schomberg's gossip, a kind of verbal 'mud' which sticks to him and drags him back to the old earth of our common origin, from which he can only finally and fully escape by the purifying, terminating fire. . . .

SCHOMBERG THE 'GOSSIP'; JONES THE 'ANTI-GENTLEMAN'

Heyst's attempts to break out of the magic circle of the islands take him in the direction either of New Guinea or Saigon—'to cannibals or to cafés'. As if to say that both modes of existence are present in the world, and, more to the point, there is not a great deal of difference between them. I have referred else-where to the importance of 'eating' in Conrad, and here, as in many other ways, he picks up a theme from *Falk,* in making Schomberg obsessed with the need for mankind to eat at his hotel: 'his ambition was to feed it at a profitable price, and his delight was to talk of it behind its back'. The bad talk is a reflex of, and connected with, the bad food: the ears and the mouth are alike malnourished there. No wonder Heyst avoids that establishment; in the event one might well opt for nature's cannibals over Schomberg's café. And Schomberg's destructive resentment starts from the fact that Heyst does not eat at his 'establishment'. Mr Jones, a 'starved spectre', intense and insatiable, rapacious and insubstantial, is a clear relative of Kurtz in *Heart of Darkness.* But for all his talk of being a 'gentleman' he knows that he is undomesticated. 'We aren't tame,' he casually warns Schomberg (who is terrified of 'ferocity'), adding 'in a voice indifferent, as if issuing from a tomb, that he depended on himself, as if the world were still one great, wild jungle without law'. Mr Jones seems deathly, his vitality exhausted, yet he still has 'the will and the power to sting—something vicious, unconquerable, and deadly'. In all of this he seems the very opposite of the other gentleman, Heyst, who, by contrast, looks 'martial' and capable of active struggle, yet is powerless to 'sting'; who has tried to renounce the lawless jungle of the world without realizing that it is quite out of his power to force it to renounce him.

There are also some odd, and potentially disturbing, similarities. We read much of Heyst's 'inertia', just as we hear a lot about Mr Jones's 'laziness'. Mr Jones assumes that he is—or was—from a similar 'social sphere' as Heyst, just as Ricardo assumes that he and Lena have similar 'origins' 'in the dregs of mankind.' Such offensive, contaminating, and usually dangerous assumptions of identity, or similarity, are common in Conrad—it is the theme of the 'unforeseen partnership', the unsolicited but unseverable alliance, or, as we may say with particular reference to *Victory* it is related to the overall theme of the uninvited guest. . . .

To be a 'guest' implies that one has accepted being 'domesticated' or 'tamed'—if only temporarily—according to the rules and codes of the house. Heyst's improbably fantastic, phantasmagoric, ferocious, and distinctly uninvited 'guests' are precisely *not* tame or tameable, and Heyst's attempts to continue to act the proper 'host' with these freaks, 'sports', anti-types, or monsters (we can describe them in many ways) show how impossible it is to maintain the conventions of 'civilization' when only one party feels obliged to abide by them. It becomes a black parody of hospitality—with parasitic scavengers trying to act as 'gentlemen' guests.

THE SIGNIFICANCE OF HEYST'S DRIFTING

Another disturbing similarity/difference concerning Heyst and Mr Jones lies in their habitual mode of motion. Though Mr Jones is prone to 'laziness', he has volition and intention, a plotting intelligence which—with the aid and support of Ricardo's 'instinctive savagery' and Pedro's 'brute force'— gives him goals, directions, aims, and ends, albeit these are of the most ruthlessly exploitative and self-profiting kind. Heyst, we remember, before he arrives at what is almost his terminal 'stagnation', chooses to 'drift'. 'He means to drift altogether and literally, body and soul, like a detached leaf drifting in the wind-currents . . . to drift without ever catching on to anything.' How he *does* catch on to something—or someone—

and how things catch on to him, with or without his assent, constitute a large part of the action of the book. But to drift without a goal; while making for some kind of detachment and invulnerability, involves a passive capitulation to the windcurrents of the world, or more generally, the driving powers of nature which, working through winds, or men or women, may push the motiveless drifter in any direction they choose. As Heyst explains: 'I had no schemes, no plans . . . I was simply moving on, while the others, perhaps, were going somewhere. An indifference as to roads and purposes makes one meeker, as it were.' Hence the irony of Heyst's getting temporarily involved in the coal-mining venture with its illusions of progress—the ' "stride forward', as he expressed it, in the general organization of the universe'. The theoretical 'stride forward' rapidly becomes a series of moves backwards, aptly illustrated in the spectacle of the 'abandoned settlement invaded by by the jungle' on Samburan, just as the large signboard advertising the progressive, enterprising presence of the 'Tropical Belt Coal Company' is slowly being reclaimed by the non-signifying, though not, therefore, insignificant, indigenous vegetation. First the enterprise goes, then the men, the buildings, finally the very 'signs' of the human, intruding presence. The equivocal aspects of 'drifting'—that it works at least two ways, bringing things in your way you wanted to avoid, even while you think you are avoiding the traps and travails of more conventional 'roads and purposes'— are clearly indicated by the fact that it is the wind-currents, and not the planning and steering of Mr Jones and his 'crew', which finally bring them to Samburan. 'The explanation lay in the two simple facts that the light winds and strong current of the Java Sea had drifted the boat about until they partly lost their bearings'. . . .

In seeking to avoid the purposive planning of men, it is impossible to avoid the unpredictable caprices of nature. Heyst drifts—only to be drifted *into*. He thinks to renounce the world—mentally: but as long as he is, has, a body, he cannot renounce participation in the world's physicality, and it will not renounce him: it plays with him, capriciously, cruelly, catastrophically. The gentleman at rest is visited by the 'gentleman at large' who travels randomly but deliberately, driven by currents of greed and aggressive spite, and purposefully but 'driftingly', driven by the winds and currents of nature.

HEYST'S FLAW: BEING TOUCHED

Heyst's 'detachment' from the world is 'not complete'. He has a flaw: he can still be 'touched'. So, despite his deep distrust of 'action', despite his sense that this is 'a world not worth touching, and perhaps not substantial enough to grasp', despite his having 'nothing worth holding on to', he is vulnerable, penetrable, 'touchable'. He has, he admits, asked himself 'in what way would life try to get hold of me?' but later says to Lena that 'when one's heart has been broken into in the way you have broken into mine, all sorts of weaknesses are free to enter'. His conviction is that 'He who forms a tie is lost.'

'Touch' is of course a key pun or ambiguity in the book. You can be 'touched' in the sense of being emotionally stirred, as when he first sees Alma, Heyst feels 'a secret touch on the heart'; or you can be 'touched', handled, 'grabbed' by any of the alien predators drifting around the world. Heyst is, of course, touched in both senses. As he is 'touched'—i.e. reached, smirched, marked, muddied, by gossip and calumny. 'Mud' provides an interesting leitmotiv in the book. Schomberg is a 'mud turtle', a creature of the slime. The nearby volcano indicts an unexpected 'mud shower' on Heyst's apparently immaculate island: while Mr Jones, at the peak of his anger with Ricardo, refers to his assistants as 'mud souls, obscene and cunning: mud bodies, too—the mud of the gutter'. Heyst thought to have 'no connection with earthly affairs and passions' and, like other Conradian quixotic idealists, he is habitually dressed in spotless white. But as he realizes, after forming the 'tie' with Alma/Lena, 'there must be a lot of the original Adam in me, after all'. Despite his mental contempt for matter and materiality, the original and originating mud of things, he himself, even Heyst, is ultimately of the earth, earthy.

> He reflected too, with the sense of making a discovery, that this primeval ancestor [i.e. Adam] is not easily repressed. The oldest voice in the world is just the one that never ceases to speak. If anybody could have silenced its imperative echoes, it should have been Heyst's father, with his contemptuous, inflexible negation of all effort; but apparently he could not. There was in the son a lot of that first ancestor who, as soon as he could uplift his muddy frame from the celestial mould, started inspecting and naming the animals of that paradise which he was so soon to lose.

The oldest ancestor, Adam, speaks through Heyst when his carefully maintained aloofness dissolves at the deep touch of desire—of attraction towards another, an instinct or 'drive' to take hold which thus precipitates him—much against his apparent 'will'—into the world of action. . . .

Heyst, the gentleman, the man of 'refinement', admits at one point that ' "I have managed to refine everything away. I've said to the Earth that bore me 'I am I and you are a shadow.' And, by Jove, it is so. But it appears that such words cannot be uttered with impunity" '. And so, at the end, we have the final 'refinement' by fire, which 'purifies everything', but leaves—'Nothing'. And so Conrad ends *his* book.

CHRONOLOGY

1856

Crimean War ends; Sigmund Freud born.

1857

Jozef Teodor Konrad Korzeniowski born; Charles Dickens publishes *Little Dorrit*.

1859

Charles Darwin publishes *On the Origin of Species*.

1860

Pony Express runs from Missouri to California; Abraham Lincoln elected president.

1861

Conrad's father, Apollo, arrested in Warsaw; Charles Dickens publishes *Great Expectations;* U.S. Civil War begins.

1862

Conrad accompanies exiled parents to Vologda, Russia.

1865

Death of Eva, Conrad's mother; rapid industrialization in United States; Abraham Lincoln assassinated.

1866

Fyodor Dostoyevsky publishes *Crime and Punishment;* Louisa May Alcott publishes *Little Women*.

1867

United States buys Alaska from Russia for $7.2 million.

1869

Moves to Kraków with father; death of Apollo; Leo Tolstoy publishes *War and Peace;* Suez Canal opened.

1870

Taught by Adam Pulman.

1872

Decides to go to sea.

1874

Leaves Poland for Marseilles to become a seaman; employed by Delestang, banker and shipper; passenger on *Mont Blanc* to Martinique in the Caribbean.

1875

Apprentice seaman on *Mont Blanc* to Caribbean.

1876

Serves as steward on *Saint Antoine;* Mark Twain publishes *The Adventures of Tom Sawyer.*

1877

Possibly involved in arms smuggling.

1878

Attempts suicide; enters British merchant navy; sails on *Mavis* for Constantinople; arrives in England for first time at Lowestoft; serves as seaman on *The Skimmer of the Seas* around British Isles.

1879

Serves as seaman on *Duke of Sutherland* to Australia and on *Europa* to Mediterranean; Ibsen publishes *A Doll's House;* Thomas Edison invents lightbulb.

1880

Serves as third mate on *Loch Etive* to Australia.

1881

Serves as second mate on *Palestine* to the Indian Ocean.

1883

Shipwrecked *Palestine* sinks; serves as mate on *Riversdale* to the Indian Ocean.

1884

Serves as second mate on *Narcissus* to Bombay; Mark Twain publishes *The Adventures of Huckleberry Finn.*

1885

Serves as second mate on *Tilkhurst* to Singapore; first skyscraper built in Chicago.

1886

Becomes a naturalized British citizen; certified a ship's captain.

1887

Serves as first mate on *Highland Forest* to Java; as mate on *Vidar* to Singapore, Borneo; and as mate on *Melita* to Bangkok.

1888

Captain of *Otago* to Sydney, Indian Ocean; first Kodak hand camera developed.

1889

Settles in London; begins writing *Almayer's Folly;* Adolf Hitler born.

1890

Assignment in Belgian Congo; passenger on *Ville de Maceio* to Congo; second in command on SS *Roi des Belges* up Congo River.

1891

Serves as first mate on *Torrens* until 1893; James Naismith invents basketball.

1895

Almayer's Folly published; meets Jessie George; Stephen Crane publishes *The Red Badge of Courage.*

1896

An Outcast of the Islands published; marries Jessie George; moves to Ivy Walls, Stanford-le-Hope, Essex.

1897

The Nigger of the 'Narcissus' published; meets Cunninghame Graham.

1898

Tales of Unrest published; collaboration with Ford Madox Ford; birth of son Borys; moves to Pent Farm, Kent; Spain cedes Guam, Puerto Rico, and the Philippines to the United States for $20 million.

1899

"Heart of Darkness" serialized; Boer War begins (ends 1902).

1900

Lord Jim published; J.B. Pinker becomes Conrad's agent.

1901

The Inheritors, coauthored with Ford, published; death of Queen Victoria.

1902

Youth: A Narrative, and Two Other Stories and *Typhoon* published; first Rose Bowl football game in United States.

1903

Typhoon and Other Stories published; *Romance,* coauthored with Ford, published; Wright brothers make first successful airplane flight at Kitty Hawk.

1904

Nostromo published; Russo-Japanese War begins (ends 1905).

1905

One Day More, a play, fails; spends four months in Montpellier, France; receives Civil List grant; Einstein publishes special theory of relativity.

1906

The Mirror of the Sea published; birth of son John; spends two months in Montpellier, France.

1907

The Secret Agent published; moves to Someries, Bedfordshire.

1908

A Set of Six published.

1909

Moves to Adington, Kent; Model T Ford first mass-produced in United States.

1910

"The Secret Sharer" published; suffers nervous breakdown; moves to Capel House, Kent; Boy Scouts of America founded.

1911

Under Western Eyes published.

1912

A Personal Record and *Twixt Land and Sea* published; *Titanic* sinks.

1914

Chance published; revisits Poland with family; caught there temporarily by outbreak of war; World War I begins in Europe; Panama Canal opens.

1915

Within the Tides and *Victory* published.

1916

Joins war effort; son Borys fights on French front.

1917

The Shadow-Line published; Russian Revolution; United States enters war.

1918

Borys wounded; armistice ends World War I; Polish republic restored.

1919

The Arrow of Gold published; moves to Oswalds, near Canterbury, Kent; Treaty of Versailles, settlement of World War I.

1920

The Rescue published; League of Nations created; transcontinental airmail begins.

1921

Notes on Life and Letters published; visits Corsica with Jessie; KDKA, Cincinnati, transmits first radio broadcast in United States.

1922

Play adaptation of *The Secret Agent* fails; Union of Soviet Socialist Republics established.

1923

Laughing Anne, a Play published; visits United States; gives reading at the home of railroad magnate Arthur James in New York.

1924

Declines knighthood; dies of heart attack on August 3; buried at Canterbury; *The Nature of a Crime,* coauthored with Ford, published.

1925

Tales of Hearsay and *Suspense* published.

1926

Last Essays published.

1927

Joseph Conrad: Life and Letters, edited by G. Jean-Aubry, published.

1928

The Sisters, unfinished work written in 1896, published.

FOR FURTHER RESEARCH

ABOUT JOSEPH CONRAD AND HIS WORKS

Walter Allen, *The English Novel: A Short Critical History.* New York: E.P. Dutton, 1955.

Jocelyn Baines, *Joseph Conrad: A Critical Biography.* New York: McGraw-Hill, n.d.

Richard Church, *The Growth of the English Novel.* New York: Barnes & Noble, 1961.

Olivia Cooledge, *Three Lives of Joseph Conrad.* Boston: Houghton Mifflin, 1972.

Frank W. Cushwa, *An Introduction to Conrad.* New York: Odyssey Press, 1933.

David Daiches, *The Novel and the Modern World.* Chicago: University of Chicago Press, 1939.

Ford Madox Ford, *Joseph Conrad: A Personal Remembrance.* New York: Ecco Press, 1924.

Dorothy Van Ghent, *The English Novel: Form and Function.* New York: Rinehart, 1953.

Adam Gillon, *Joseph Conrad.* Boston: Twayne, 1982.

Albert Guerard, *Conrad the Novelist.* Cambridge, MA: Harvard University Press, 1958.

Leo Gurko, *The Two Lives of Joseph Conrad.* New York: Thomas Y. Crowell, 1965.

Gerard Jean-Aubry, *The Sea Dreamer: A Definitive Biography of Joseph Conrad.* Garden City, NY: Doubleday, 1957.

Frederick R. Karl, *The Contemporary English Novel.* New York: Farrar, Straus & Giroux, 1962.

———, *Joseph Conrad: The Three Lives: A Biography.* New York: Farrar, Straus & Giroux, 1979.

Jeffrey Meyers, *Joseph Conrad: A Biography.* New York: Charles Scribner's Sons, 1991.

Marvin Mudrick, *Conrad: A Collection of Critical Essays.* Englewood Cliffs, NJ: Prentice-Hall, 1966.

Zdzislaw Najder, *Joseph Conrad: A Chronicle.* New Brunswick, NJ: Rutgers University Press, 1984.

S. Diana Neill, *A Short History of the English Novel.* London: Jerrolds, 1951.

William Lyon Phelps, *The Advance of the English Novel.* New York: Dodd, Mead, 1916.

Bertrand Russell, *Portraits from Memory and Other Essays.* New York: Simon and Schuster, 1956.

Daniel R. Schwarz, *Conrad: Almayer's Folly to Under Western Eyes.* Ithaca, NY: Cornell University Press, 1980.

George Stade, ed., *Six Modern British Novelists.* New York: Columbia University Press, 1974.

J.I.M. Stewart, *Eight Modern Writers.* Oxford: Clarendon Press, 1963.

ABOUT CONRAD'S TIMES

James Truslow Adams, *Empire on the Seven Seas: The British Empire 1784–1939.* New York: Charles Scribner's Sons, 1940.

Arthur Bryant, *Pageant of England 1840–1940.* New York: Harper and Brothers, 1941.

———, *Spirit of England.* London: Collins, 1982.

C.E. Carrington and J. Hampden Jackson, *A History of England.* Cambridge, England: Cambridge University Press, 1945.

Alfred F. Havighurst, *Twentieth-Century Britain.* 2nd ed. New York: Harper and Row, 1962.

Carlton J.H. Hayes and Margareta Faissler, *Modern Times.* New York: Macmillan, 1966.

T.L. Jarman, *A Short History of Twentieth-Century England.* London: Blandford Press, 1963.

Marjorie and C.H.B. Quennell, *A History of Everyday Things in England, 1851–1914.* Vol. 4. London: B.T. Batsford, 1934.

Stephen W. Sears, ed., *The Horizon History of the British Empire.* New York: American Heritage, 1973.

G.M. Trevelyan, *History of England.* Vol. 3. Garden City, NY: Doubleday Anchor, 1926.

R.J. White, *The Horizon Concise History of England.* New York: American Heritage, 1971.

ORGANIZATIONS TO CONTACT

Joseph Conrad Society of America
c/o Professor Raymond Brebach
Drexel University
Department of Humanities
Philadelphia, PA 19104
(215) 895-2446
e-mail: brebach@duvm.ocs.drexel.edu

The society publishes the semiannual newsletter *Joseph Conrad Today*, abstracts of papers, lectures, meeting announcements, and book reviews.

WORKS BY JOSEPH CONRAD

Almayer's Folly (1895)

An Outcast of the Islands (1896)

The Nigger of the 'Narcissus' (1897)

Tales of Unrest (1898)

Lord Jim, a Tale (1900)

The Inheritors, an Extravagant Story, coauthor Ford (1901)

Youth: A Narrative, and Two Other Stories, includes "Heart of Darkness," serialized in 1899 (1902)

Typhoon (1902)

Typhoon and Other Stories (1903)

Romance, coauthor Ford (1903)

Nostromo, a Tale of the Seaboard (1904)

The Mirror of the Sea, Memories and Impressions (1906)

The Secret Agent, a Simple Tale (1907)

A Set of Six (1908)

Under Western Eyes, a Novel (1911)

Some Reminiscences, also known as *A Personal Record* (1912)

Twixt Land and Sea, Tales (1912)

Chance, a Tale in Two Parts (1913)

One Day More, a Play in One Act (1913)

Within the Tides (1915)

Victory, an Island Tale (1915)

The Shadow-Line, a Confession (1917)

The Arrow of Gold, a Story Between Two Notes (1919)

The Rescue: A Romance of the Shallows (1920)

Notes on Life and Letters (1921)

The Secret Agent, Drama in Four Acts, adaption of the novel (1921)

The Rover (1923)

Laughing Anne, a Play (1923)

The Nature of a Crime, coauthor Ford, written in 1908 (1924)

Suspense, a Napoleonic Novel, unfinished (1925)

Tales of Hearsay (1925)

Last Essays (1926)

The Sisters, written in 1896, unfinished (1928)

INDEX